RUPTURE IN THE CANVAS

The hidden doorway to your Soul's evolution

RUPTURE IN THE CANVAS

The hidden doorway to your Soul's evolution

Nancy Willbern, PhD

atmosphere press

© 2025 Nancy Willbern

Published by Atmosphere Press

Cover design by Matthew Fielder

No part of this book may be reproduced without permission from the author except in brief quotations and in reviews.

Atmospherepress.com

*This book is dedicated with heartfelt gratitude
to the Great Artist—
my inspiration and my muse*

*...and to that elusive Dave Bair—
the stranger I recognized.*

CONTENTS

INVOCATION	1
PREFACE	3
INTRODUCTION	8
THE FIRST RUPTURE	19
1: My Fate	21
2: The Fated Dance	40
3: I Died. I Live.	53
4: From Fate to Destiny	64
A DEEPER LOOK #1	75
5: The Treasure	77
THE SECOND RUPTURE	85
6: Flying Solo	87
7: White Stones in the Moonlight	98
8: Life Lesson	110
9: Unlikely Messenger	120

THE THIRD, FOURTH & FIFTH RUPTURES   127

    10: Splintered Pieces   129

    11: Promise Made   142

    12: Memorial Day   151

    13: Promise Kept   159

A DEEPER LOOK #2   169

    14: Forgiveness   171

THE SIXTH RUPTURE   183

    15: The Little Secret   185

    16: The Choice   193

    17: In and Out of the Box   200

    18: A True Love Story   210

A DEEPER LOOK #3   221

    19: A Bird's-Eye View   223

    20: A Parting Gift   237

APPENDIX   243
REFERENCES   255
ACKNOWLEDGMENTS   257

*There is only one essential question:
Is the universe a friendly place? This is the first
and most basic question all people must
answer for themselves.*

Albert Einstein

AUTHOR'S NOTE

The writing of one's personal story will inevitably include stories of others whose lives have intersected with the author's. While writing *Rupture in the Canvas*, I have tried my best to tell the truth from my perspective while being respectful and compassionate to all involved. *Please note that some names and identifying details have been altered to protect anonymity.* Other than that, I have stayed close to the actual storyline as I experienced it. No doubt, others would have their own version of our shared story. Although I'm sure there would be plenty of overlap, we all live in different life-movies. And this movie depiction is decidedly mine.

INVOCATION

*Something watches over us and we know it when
we follow the little voice inside or heed the warning
or inspiration that arrives as if on wings.*

*We need the intermediaries that keep us close to
the spirit of life, to the wonders of nature
and to the subtleties of our own inner nature.*

- Michael Meade -

There is a quiet, open space inside myself where I often hear the Voice. Sometimes it speaks to me when I ask a direct question. Other times it comes in the form of a vision or as a character in a dream, personified as an Angel, or a Guide, or a Soul Keeper. Sometimes I just feel its presence in my body. Regardless of its presentation, I don't experience it as *my* voice and it's not a voice that is audible out there in the world. This other Voice, this other Viewpoint, does not come from the part of me I identify with most of the time, which lives on a roller coaster of felt sensations and heartfelt emotions. That's the me I identify with most of the time. This other Voice of the "Divine Ones," this other energy, is always bigger and broader, deeper and steadier, more peaceful, more wholistic in its vantage point. And it is that bigger-than vantage point that I have come to rely upon.

After living years out of my own best thinking, there came a time when I was compelled to let go and venture beyond the boundaries of my habits of mind. Thankfully, that compulsion has come again and again.

So, I am bringing you with me, my Reader Friend, into that sometimes terrifying, sometimes delicious *liminal space* that is neither here nor there, physical nor ephemeral, fact nor illusion—the dark, mysterious, transformational chrysalis of the human experience.

I hope you will stay long enough to take this adventure into the unknown with me. I hope you will be willing to set your rational thinking aside long enough to step right past the boundary of your known reality, right past the borderland of the you that you know yourself to be. Because that's what this whole book is about: trusting enough to step into that exquisite place that lies just past the expected and into the birthplace of all unfettered creativity, the sacred space in the center of your heart.

PREFACE

The greatest privilege of a human life
is to become a midwife to the awakening
of the soul in another person.

- Plato -

I have been a transpersonal psychotherapist working in private practice for thirty years, but my interest in the uniqueness of humans began way back in high school, which for me was many, many years ago. I have been enthralled with human growth and development since taking Mrs. Verdene Ryder's Child Development class in my senior year. It sparked in me an unexpected fascination for all that it means to be human. But when I step into it and look a little deeper, I can see that my captivation is founded first in that universal miracle of nature that allows a fully-grown oak tree—massive trunk, broad branching limbs, prickly dark green leaves—to live inside its incubating protective covering as a pre-existent template of itself. How is it that, in some mysterious way, the oak tree is already there within the acorn? I love that!

I confess that I'm in love with the evolutionary life force that compels all living forms to emerge from the deep soil, blossom into bloom, break out of their shells to become more of what they were meant to be all along. I'm in love with its symmetry of form, its spiraling outward from center to periphery, its predictability of pattern, as well as its honoring of the uniqueness of each frond or feather or forelock. I'm spellbound by its organic emergence and expansion, the increasing complexity embedded in all of nature's varieties, but when it comes to humans, the passion swells all the more. With humans, it's not just about the predictable emergence of hair and hand and heart, but the evolutionary dawning of consciousness, of meaning-making, of an awakening of awareness of self in relation to all that surrounds it. That pinnacle of nature is worth the fascination of a lifetime. At least, it has been for me.

I took my newly discovered fervor for human growth and development to college with me and decided to major in it. Although my interest in it refined and expanded over all my years of schooling, I stayed true to it through my doctorate in Developmental Psychology. My interest morphed from a focus on children to adult development in general to a more specific and in-depth focus on the evolution of the self and consciousness, which, as you might have guessed already, is the underlying topic of this book.

In the final year of my doctoral program, I took a course that forever changed the way I see the world. I was invited by the professor, along with about nine other students, to take his seminar on Post-Piagetian Theory. The professor was Dr. Philip Powell, a most remarkable, eclectic hodge-podge of a person. He was a very large African American who, by the time I met him walked with a cane. In his teenage years, however, Powell served as a warlord for a gang in the most gang-populated city in the U.S.—Chicago. As he matured and moved into higher education, exposed to more of the world, Powell heard the call to become a man of God. He was ordained as a Baptist minister, all the while practicing the eight-fold path of a Buddhist. He was also a Mensa-certified genius.

The focus of the class was a description of what is possible past the boundary of Jean Piaget's[1] final stage of cognitive

---

[1] Jean Piaget is the developmental theorist who mapped out the predictable stages of Cognitive Development: sensorimotor (birth to two

development, which he labeled formal operations. This is the level of thought where we can think abstractly, reason logically, and solve problems using hypothetical situations. What was so fascinating about this next level of development, post-formal operations, was that it didn't emerge organically along an ever-widening spiral, like most of the earlier stages. Instead, its entry point was some sort of life-altering experience—an event that jolted the person out of her habituated way of thinking, past all previous assumptions about the nature of reality, an event that separated her from her sense of self. That type of experience has the power to leave a person flailing in a free fall. And that is the perfect blank space for something new to emerge. That something new is a never-before-experienced, unbiased take on reality, one that is more experiential and more wholistic than a formal operational level of thought. When a person surrenders into that nothingness, they have the opportunity to move out of a strictly personal experience of self into what is called a trans-personal experience.

An unbiased, transpersonal take on reality is not easily put into a linear description, so Powell pointed to this hard-to-describe new realm by having us read about the experiences of people who had gone through it themselves. We read books written by authors who lived in that level of awareness like Marcus Aurelius' *Meditations* and Thomas Berry's *The Great Work*. We read about the life and works of Gandhi, Martin Luther King, Jr and the ground-breaking, Gestalt therapist, Barry Stevens. We were not only learning about the post-formal, transpersonal level of consciousness; we were getting a feel for it.

At the same time I was taking Powell's class, I was writing my dissertation. It was a qualitative research project in which I interviewed people who had gone through a life-changing event, meaning that before the event they thought of them-

---

years), preoperational thinking (two to seven years), concrete operational thinking (seven to eleven years), and formal operational thinking (eleven years onward).

selves as one person but after the event experienced themselves as someone new. I wanted to find out if their sense of identity was altered, would their personal God-image be altered as well? It turns out it would.

Here's the irony of it all. While I was writing about other people who had undergone a life-changing event, and while I was taking Powell's class on Post-Piagetian theory, I had my own life-shattering experience—the breaking open of my marriage of twenty-one years. I now had a firsthand, up-close-and-personal experience of all that we had been learning about in Powell's class. I got it on a cellular level. As a result, I decided to include my own crushing experience as part of my dissertation. I shared my experience right along with all the subjects I had interviewed. That was when I first began to write about my own life in relation to this jarring, miracle moment embedded in the process of human evolution.

* * *

In some way that my rational mind can't wrap itself around, humans are also born with our truer, more authentic, and evolved identities tucked secretly inside just like the mighty oak swaddled inside the acorn. But unlike the oak or our furry and feathered friends, we get to engage with the unfolding. We have been granted the gift of choice to participate in that emergence or not. And that is the most magnificent gift of all.

This book is about that uniquely human gift of choice: to make the humbling and often terrifying decision to surrender all that we have known and believed to be true, thereby exposing a secret treasure trove beyond what we might have imagined.

It is that uniquely human moment of choice where my becoming a transpersonal psychotherapist dovetails into my fascination with the evolution of human consciousness. I didn't come into the world of therapy through the lens of pathology. When clients come in to see me as a therapist aching from an unexpected and, more often than not, greatly unwanted occurrence in their lives, I don't see them as simply neurotic or maladjusted. I see them in the middle of one of the most exciting life events a human being can experience. They are in transition. They're going through an initiation into a new reality, a rite of passage, a death, and a rebirth, all at once. And I see my job as a doula, holding their hands, reminding them to breathe, reassuring them through every step of the way, "I know. This pain *sucks*! It's god-awful! But, trust me, it's taking you somewhere entirely new. And I don't want you to miss it."

INTRODUCTION

Between stimulus and response, there is a space.
And in that space is our power to choose.
It's in that choice that comes
our growth and freedom.

- Viktor Frankl -

I crumpled to the floor and scrunched myself into a fetal position next to the skirt of our king-sized bed. "I don't want you!" I screamed at God, tears streaming down my cheeks, snot running from my nose. I didn't care. A surge of anger and angst, terror and desperation rose from my stomach, tore through my heart and out of my throat, emerging as convulsing sobs. "I don't want you!" I shouted again. The words were absorbed by my gasping, my inability to breathe. I felt a wrenching stab run all the way through the core of my body. I took one more deep breath and shouted again, "I don't want you! I want him!"

But I didn't have him. And hadn't for a very long time.

* * *

That moment was the most devastating moment of my life. It left me completely undone, severed from the only *me* I had known myself to be. In that one excruciating moment, *I* was no more and the time-honored reality that I lived in was blown to bits. I was sent flailing out into nothingness, terrified, shocked beyond belief, speechless, rudderless, lost—so utterly lost without any sense of direction.

So, what are we to do when some unimaginable life event ruptures our picture of reality, blows our minds, and breaks our hearts? What are we to do when something impossible arises to not only take away a job or a loved one or our health, but shatters who we know ourselves to be, shreds the very fiber of our being—not just rendering us unrecognizable, but untethered from all of our identity touchstones? Or what about when an unexpected event rattles us senseless with some mind-blowing, heart-opening grace? Wrestling with these hardest of human questions is the central theme of this book.

The Premise

Rupture in the Canvas focuses on a divinely designed paradox organically hidden within the human condition. Who knew that a seemingly isolated, unimaginable life event is actually the climatic tipping point within an evolutionary unfolding? What we initially experience as shocking—often painfully disastrous, other times astonishingly delightful, but always disorienting—can become the entryway into an experience of reality that we didn't even know existed and certainly didn't know we wanted. This surprising revelation does not come to us through a cognitive shift in perception; rather, it comes through an undeniable, full-bodied jolt. It is at that bombshell moment that life presents us with a choice to either let it have its way with us or to resist it with a screaming "NOOO!"

Admittedly, most of us start with the "NOOO!" That reaction is to be expected and deserves to be honored. It needs to be given the time and the space to have its full say. If, however, we can stay somewhat alert and can bring in the slightest scrap of trust, we are presented with the greatest bone-rattling responsibility and the most grace-filled privilege that we as humans can experience: the choice to expand our consciousness by participating in our own continued evolution—or not. *Rupture in the Canvas* is about that choice.

The Organization

The complexity of the human psyche and how it evolves is not easily captured in a string of words. I am grateful a more accessible description was brought to me in a revelatory dream that I call *The Great Artist Dream*. The Dream confronts us with a moving-picture-style portrayal of the choice we are left with when we experience the unimaginable. As it also forms the framework for the developmental path I present in this book, I include it here in its entirety.

The Great Artist Dream

My friend Maggie and I were invited to study under The Great Artist. We had heard about this remarkable teacher from a group of our friends who had already studied under him. So, when our invitations arrived, we were thrilled.

The dream opens as we enter the reception area of the warehouse studio, a rather nondescript space—four beige walls, a gray concrete floor, meandering cracks splintering its surface like tiny tributaries from a river out of view.

To our left was a pasty-white man sitting at a fold-out table. We immediately recognized him as a bookkeeper. His features and actions were so predictable that he was a caricature of himself, wearing thick bifocals and a green sun visor to deflect the glare from his adjustable table lamp. Ignoring our arrival, the bookkeeper stayed focused on calculating figures on an archaic adding machine. Lined on the table in front of him were rows and rows of what looked like receipts. It began to dawn on Maggie and me that each receipt represented a different life experience—

of ours. We realized that this inhospitable, key-clacking man was doing an accounting of our lives. As we looked on, the calculator tape began to lengthen and curl over the edge of the table. In my mind, the clacking keys tapped in cadence with the familiar nursery rhyme...

> "There was a little girl who had a little curl that sat
> in the middle of her forehead.
> And when she was good,
> she was very, very good,
> but when she was bad, she was horrid."

The longer the calculator tape grew, adding curl after curl, the more foreboding the space became. We stood there trembling like children as the cloying aura in the room clutched and suffocated.

Just then, The Great Artist pushed through the large swinging doors at the far end of the room. His buoyant energy burst into the tightening grip of the foyer like the swoosh of a magic wand. Oh, relief! Delight! It felt as if he had just rescued us from the jaws of some ravenous beast.

The Great Artist was tall and thin, wearing round, wire-rimmed reading glasses perched on the end of his nose. Despite his advanced age, he carried himself with amazing agility, sleeves rolled up, artist apron splattered with acrylics. This man was alive!

"Oh, you're here!" he exclaimed as he blew through the doors. "Ready to come on back?"

Maggie and I both looked in the direction of the bookkeeper, still busy with his computations, those punishing calculator keys clacking in the background.

Smiling, The Great Artist reassured us, "Oh, you don't have to wait on all that accounting stuff. That's just to keep the bookkeeper busy and happy."

Whew! Our pent-up anxiety melted as new air infiltrated the room. Without hesitation, I followed The Great Artist through the large swinging doors into the studio we had heard so much about. Maggie followed close behind.

The pungent scent of paint, turpentine, and linseed oil startled our senses as we entered the cavernous room, but what took our breath away was IT, the infamous collage foretold to us by our friends, the former students. Let me just quickly say that hearing about the enormous painting didn't compare to the actual sight of it up close. We couldn't help but stand there in jaw-dropping awe in its presence.

Across the entire back wall was the largest canvas we had ever seen. Painted on it was everything—everything possibly imaginable. The mural was a virtual collage of reality and fantasy all mixed together. There were people, all kinds of people—black, white, brown people, tall people and skinny people, short and fat people. There were landscapes and dragons, skyscrapers and spiderwebs, trolls hiding under bridges, ornate calligraphy and geometric shapes, starbursts shining through midnight skies, long-trunked elephants and long-necked giraffes with monkeys riding on their backs. There were animated stick figures, Picasso-like abstracts, and Monet-muted hillsides painted right next to devouring monsters stalking their prey while three good fairies fluttered overhead. There were tornados and landslides, tsunamis and earthquakes, happy children, starving children, rabid dogs, and castles twinkling in the moonlight. There were fat, woolly sheep grazing in bucolic pastures, grimy subways traveling under bustling city streets, and astronauts flying to the moon. There were mathematical equations, birthday cakes glowing with candles, sunbeams shining through ocean waves, computer screens flashing marketing slogans, and sunsets layered in orange and lavender, violet and deep red fading into the palest of pink. The energy of this piece was palpable, visceral. It was magnetic. We stood transfixed in shock and awe at its horror and its beauty; at its completeness.

While we stood gazing at the mural, our mentor gathered art supplies for us from his personal workspace, a massive, paint-encrusted wooden art table covered in decades worth of creative tools. Brushes stood up straight, soaking in glasses of cloudy water. Tubes and tubes of acrylics in every color—sky-blue and lime-green, bright yellow and crimson-red, orange, lavender, and mauve—all housed in rows and rows of cardboard boxes.

The Great Artist supplied each of us with a tall stool, a set of acrylics, paint brushes of various sizes, an artist's palette, and aprons. He seated us a few feet apart, each in front of a blank space on the canvas. These blank spaces were to be our spaces, reserved just for Maggie and me to paint whatever we chose. Well, not exactly. The Great Artist's assignment was for each of us to paint an image that would best represent the deepest, most unique expression of who we believed ourselves to be. He didn't care what we painted or how well we painted, he explained. All that he cared about was, "Does this represent your truest expression of who you are, what you value in life? Does it jump out and say, 'Maggie!' or 'Nancy!' when you see it?"

Maggie and I sat perched on our stools and entered earnest, concentrated thought, each trying to sort through all the possible versions of ourselves. "Maybe I'm best depicted as this or, no, maybe that," we thought, trying on each one. We worked hard, each of us taking our assigned task seriously.

As we sat there pondering, brushes in hand, The Great Artist walked back over to his workbench, picked up an X-Acto knife and, without any warning, walked over to the giant collage and slashed through the canvas from the top left corner all the way down and across the bottom, leaving a gaping, garish gash. In abject horror, Maggie gasped and screamed out, "NOOO!" Inside myself, I felt just like she did: shocked, heartbroken, and devastated beyond belief. I felt disoriented and confused. Most of all, I felt betrayed. With that one dramatic stroke, he had ruined everything. "NOOO!" Maggie screamed again.

I did not scream. I sat there on my barstool, holding my breath, stunned, wordlessly trying to make sense of what had just happened, and then looked up into The Great Artist's face. He was smiling down at me, a twinkle in his eye. "So, what are you going to do with that?" he asked. I kept looking into his deep, blue, trustworthy eyes, leading me to question the apparent destructiveness of his devastating action. Maggie didn't move. She sat on her stool, transfixed on the gaping hole in the canvas, frozen in disbelief.

Keeping his gaze on me, The Great Artist asked again, "What are you going to do with that, Nancy?" I was surprised he called me by name. As his question lingered in the air, The Great Artist pushed the yielding flap caused by the tear, held it open as if it were a doorway, and nodded his head in the direction of the exposed blackness behind the canvas.

The effects of this gesture cascaded through every cell in my body. In one timeless nanosecond, my universe flipped from upside down to right side up, as if I had been sailing a great clipper ship with the mast underwater, and the thing had just righted itself. That one nod of the head launched a series of tidal waves, shooting sheets of ocean spray high into the sky. The mast rose to the surface and centered itself, tall and proud, sails billowing in the generous wind. It was cataclysmic and at the same time a most unexpected, glorious surprise. It suddenly felt like the punchline to a benevolent cosmic joke.

With that one simple gesture, in a moment out of time, I morphed from stunned confusion into curious wonder. The gaping rupture in the canvas was not just about its destruction. It was about an invitation to someplace more, someplace beyond my deepest, best, most intentional thinking, beyond where my imagination could even take me. It was about an adventure into the unknown, led by The Great Artist himself. I could go or I could stay. The choice was all mine.

I took a deep breath and stepped through the rupture in the canvas.

The Dream as Roadmap

The Great Artist Dream came to me some seven years after I found myself huddled on the floor next to my king-sized bed, shouting at God. That gut-wrenching moment marked the beginning of my waking up to the truth of my broken marriage. Years later, this really big, awe-inspiring *Dream* sailed in through the night and gifted me with a moving-picture-style summary of the whole process I had been trying to understand for the previous seven years. I couldn't help but recognize the *Dream* as an incredible, elegant integration of all that I had gone through in relation to that first jagged **Rupture in My Canvas**. I felt gifted by its clarity, its wholistic completeness. All the pieces finally fell into place.

I now, some thirty years later, recognize that *The Great Artist Dream* offers much more than just an integration of all that *I* experienced with my first major **Rupture**. Its characters, spaces, transitions between those spaces, and the direction of movement within the *Dream* provide a roadmap to understanding the evolutionary process that becomes available to any of us, with each life-altering rip in our **Canvas**. It presents all the aspects of the self that come into play when our lives are torn apart: our fear-based **Maggie** who screams in defiance, who remains fixated on the defiled **Canvas**; our **Nancy** who carries a sense of personal agency, who claims her right to choose. Of course, there is **The Great Artist** who represents a personification of the Creative Life-Force, who continues to invite us into more of who we were always meant to be. Then there is the life-sucking trio that lives in the **Foyer** that I now refer to as the **Hungry Ghosts**, consisting of the calculator-clacking **Bookkeeper** and his two invisible but palpable sidekicks from my own life—the **Protector**, who constantly demands that I try harder, and the **Preacher**, whose job it is to scare the hell out of me. (Your inner characters may be entirely different from mine.) Finally, the *Dream* alludes to the **Soul** who shows up the minute we decide to step through the **Rupture in the Canvas**. She represents the aspect of the self that is willing to interact with life directly, no longer mediated through concepts, or expectations, or beliefs.

The spaces in the *Dream* are integral to the map as well: the **Foyer** with all of its foreboding energies, the **Studio**, which offers opportunity, the **Canvas**, which holds all of the images on the **Collective Collage** as well as the blank spaces where more images can be added; the paradoxical **Rupture**, which represents destruction as well as freedom; and, finally, the **Space Behind the Canvas**, which leads into the great unknown. The transitions between those spaces (the swinging double doors that lead into the **Studio**, the artist stations in front of the blank spaces on the **Collective Collage**, and the space created by the **Rupture in the Canvas**) and the direction of movement within the *Dream* (from the **Foyer** to the **Studio** through the **Rupture** into the **Space Behind the Canvas**) all serve as vital components of the roadmap to the evolutionary process that becomes available to anyone who has experienced a life-changing event. As such, *The Great Artist Dream* will serve as the organizing thread that runs throughout the text. I will refer to it often. (*The Dream as Roadmap* is described in full detail in the Appendix. Please refer to it for clarification as you read through the text.)

The Perspective

Rupture in the Canvas is a description of my professional understanding of the relationship between life-changing events and the evolution of consciousness, as illustrated by my personal encounters with it. Over the course of seventeen years, I experienced six major life-altering events, including a devastating divorce, a prophetic message from a past life, miraculous connections with my father as he declined into dementia and at the moment of his death, and the eventual claiming of a forbidden love. Amid the storytelling, I point out how the elements of *The Great Artist Dream* appear and are repeated again and again through each unique **Rupture**. Taken as a whole, this series of life events exposes the arc of evolution as a non-linear spiral that moves out from the center and then circles back around again and again. Lessons are learned with each new encounter and are then repeated as new ones intermittently emerge.

Clearly, my educational training and professional experience have not prevented me from crawling through my own painful rites of passage. We are all aware that knowing how to read a map is not the same as trudging through the terrain. While my training and all the years of private practice don't buffer me from the pain of being human, they do enable me to describe those painful passages from an informed perspective. I can recognize what is happening to my clients and, over time, even to myself within an evolutionary framework. My training allows me to know a little bit about how all the moving parts work together as a whole, rather than just isolated, unexpected occurrences.

In the chapters that follow, I will be sharing with you all of the very human ways the different parts of me have responded to **The Great Artist's** invitations throughout my life in relation to the restrictive energies experienced in the **Foyer**, the opportunities offered in the **Studio**, and the variety of responses I have had to my own heart-stopping, mind-blowing events—the times I crumpled to the floor, the times I defiantly rebelled, and the times I dared to venture through the **Ruptures** in my own **Canvas**.

I hope that by reading about how all the elements in *The Great Artist Dream* have been animated in my life, you might recognize them animating in yours. Perhaps you're able to see where you are on the map, which room you live in most of the time, and which *Dream* characters you seem to relate to. My hope is that sharing my story might help you to experience *your* story more deeply, more clearly, more compassionately—more consciously—and with a little more trust.

THE FIRST RUPTURE

CHAPTER ONE

MY FATE

*Fate shapes the particular plotline
through which each soul tries to awaken
and enter the great
drama of life.*

- Michael Meade -

WHERE IT ALL BEGAN

From all outward appearances, my upbringing was about as plain-vanilla, non-glam boring as it could have been for a Texas girl from the suburbs. If you're old enough, think: *Donna Reed, Father Knows Best, Leave It to Beaver*. If you're not, stream them to find out what suburban, Anglo-Saxon American life was like in the 1950s and early 60s. Those old TV series are the CliffsNotes of my childhood. The seemingly innocuous, white-washed society that emerged after WWII is why the *Make Love, Not War* philosophy of the late 60s erupted. Coming from that culture, the mounting outcry on college campuses against the Vietnam War was one of the first collective uprisings against an external authority that expected conformity. The rebellion of the late 1960s and 70s broke the spell that the post-war 50s held over us. As a collective, it was our coming-of-age moment. And that's when *Father Knows Best* was replaced with *Laugh-In*. Thank God!

To any outside observer, my sheltered, domesticated growing-up years appeared to be wholesome, safe, and secure, and in many ways, they were. There was much to be appreciated in that steady, mundane existence. We lived in a white clapboard, three-bedroom house in Bellaire, a bedroom community to the wider Houston metroplex. Brick-and-mortar planter boxes ran across the front of the house, filled with rows of red geraniums that burst into bloom in April before dying off in the August heat. At night, we slept with our screened-in windows open, fans whirring. We never locked our doors even when we left to go out somewhere, which was most often either church, our grandparents' house, or Weingarten's, the neighborhood grocery store.

The neighborhood swimming pool was built just across the street. To get there, my sisters and I ran through the asphalt parking lot, our dime-store rubber flip-flops sticking to its tarry surface, flap-flap-flapping with each prancing step. On humid summer nights, we skipped behind the mosquito-fumigator trucks like Celtic goddesses emerging through the mists of Avalon.

My two older sisters, Betsy and Robyn, were only two and a half years apart. I am four and a half years younger than Robyn and seven years younger than Betsy. I was the baby of our immediate family, the third daughter, as well as the baby of our extended family on my father's side. I was the sixth granddaughter of only granddaughters and the last chance to carry on the family name. So, when I die, so goes the name.

Betsy and Robyn shared a bedroom. I had my own. They put their bookcases down the center of the room to create a clear demarcation between "hers" and "mine." Their personalities were like oil and water. Sometimes they mixed in harmony like a fine vinaigrette. Other times, they repelled each other, not ever really understanding much less appreciating the other's inherent unique differences. Betsy was an introvert, her nose always in a book, while Robyn came onto the planet with a big splash, a wide smile, and a loud voice that would not be ignored. I always fell somewhere in between.

Although a star debater and a graduate from Rice University (double major in Biology and Philosophy), our mother, like other mothers of her generation, stayed home to raise her girls. She would be at the house every day when we got home from school. She set the daily rhythm with her three home-cooked meals. Mama provided a trustworthy home base. She was "home" to us.

Before I started school, our father, who we Southern girls forever called "Daddy," worked a nine-to-five job down at the ship channel during the day and went to law school at night. He always got home by 5:30 to sit down at our Early American round maple table to have dinner with the family. At the sound of his familiar three-note "Daddy's-home whistle," I'd run as fast as my toddler legs could take me, screaming "Daddy! Daddy! Daddy!" to greet him at the door. He'd hear my bare feet padding over the brick-patterned linoleum, hold out his arms, and pick me up over his head, familiar Old Spice wafting through the air as his warm bass voice declared, "Nancer!" with genuine delight. And for one breathtaking moment every day, we were held in a circle of we-ness, just Daddy and me, two notes in a love song. Our love song.

This series of formative snapshots—my sheltered, suburban upbringing in the 50s, held safe and secure by Mama's forever presence, my being the youngest of a whole line-up of daughters, and me as a toddler racing to meet Daddy at the door when he got home from work—are noteworthy images painted on my *Collective Collage* in *The Great Artist's Studio*. Those frozen-in-time images and the meanings I attached to them played a major part in formulating my early worldview and emerging self-image.

* * *

Jungian analyst and lover of myth, Michael Meade makes a clear distinction between two words that we often use interchangeably: fate and destiny. He explains that a person's collection of childhood snapshots and the idiosyncratic meanings attached to them make up our *fate*. Our fate is how we experience our lives when we are unconsciously playing out our childhood programming. In *The Great Artist Dream*, my fate is depicted in both the life-limiting energies in the **Foyer** as well as all of the images that are painted on the **Collective Collage** on the back wall of the **Studio**. **Maggie** represents my fated-self. She is fear-based and careful and tries ever so hard to be perfect and good. There is nothing new or creative or adventurous about my **Maggie-self**. She stays under the authority of the suffocating **Three Hungry Ghosts**.

By contrast, we activate our destiny whenever we decide to step out of the constraints of our fateful experiences. According to Meade, we are born with our destiny hidden inside our **Souls**, like the oak tree that somehow lives inside the acorn. With humans, the unfolding of that destiny does not happen automatically as it does with the oak. We have both the privilege and the responsibility to choose its emergence or not. In the *Great Artist Dream*, I move toward my destiny whenever I step into the **Studio** as my **Nancy-self** ready to paint some images of my own, but most poignantly when I dare to step through the **Rupture in the Canvas**. This launches me into my truest identity, my **Soul-self**.

* * *

Formative snapshots don't stop for any of us in our preschool years. In my life, there were many more to come. I am not exaggerating when I say that from all outward appearances, my family looked about as picture-perfect as anyone could imagine in the 1950s and 60s. There wasn't a lot of drama, no shouting or slamming of doors, no drug or alcohol abuse. Ha! No drug or alcohol *use* at all, for that matter. We had our typical squabbles and power struggles, but big picture, my sisters and I were well loved and cared for.

My parents loved to debate over the dinner table, but as soon as it turned from a stimulating exchange of opinions to an emotional reaction, the debate would end with my mother making one distinct tap with her fork on her plate and saying with obvious disdain, "Roy." And that would be that. The conversation stopped and we all felt uncomfortable. By and large, everybody was pretty respectful of everybody else. We all colored within the lines, so to speak, which was the norm of the mainstream culture during that time, at least on the surface of things.

After WWII, folks settled down into traditional roles. Conformity was the expectation. It was believed to lead to stability and homogeneity, which must have felt comforting and safe after a war had been waged across the whole revolving planet. Along with so many others, my family fit into that over-culture pattern. And it is true; for a while, we all did feel pretty safe and secure within that prescribed value system. For a time, we were held within a kind of bubble of innocence that, from our present-day vantage point, we can see was destined to burst. And that bubble did burst, first on the national level with the escalation of the Cold War in the mid-1950s and then later with the rise of the counterculture consciousness-raising of the late 1960s.

In my family, our particular bubble of innocence ruptured with the convergence of two hidden fault lines that ran surreptitiously underneath our otherwise got-it-all-together, all-American family facade. One came in like a tsunami and the other seeped in like a toxic vapor.

The Tsunami

In the summer of 1952, just a few months before I turned two, my mother's mother, Cora—renamed "Poco" by her granddaughters—developed a benign but painful cyst on the optic nerve of her right eye. The surgeons debated whether to remove the eye or to go in through the skull to extract the cyst. They opted for the latter. That's right. They opted for brain surgery in 1952. My grandmother woke up from the surgery with a quarter of her skull permanently removed, calling out for her mother who had died giving birth to her.

And there it was. In that one instant, it was as if the Earth's tectonic plates shifted deep under the ocean, causing a tsunami to barrel through our family's placid existence with its gale winds and explosive tides. None of us was ever the same. Our habituated roles and familiar positions were ravished out of place. Overnight, my grandfather Daddy Ben lost his beloved wife and became her devoted caretaker. My mother quit her short-lived job as a biology teacher to become the family matriarch and helpmate to her father, who lived just ten minutes away. Still in law school at night, Daddy resumed the full financial weight of the family with no option for relief from our mom. My oldest sister Betsy became a straight-A student and Robyn, the middle child, coped by bringing us comic relief. I just did my best to stay still and quiet, to be as invisible as possible, not wanting to add any more waves to our storm-ravaged lifeboat. As for my grandmother—she was forever banished to a netherworld, not fully here yet not fully there either.

After her surgery, none of us were prepared for what was to come. My grandfather's way of coping was to treat my grandmother as if nothing had changed. We followed his lead, acting as if there had been no gale winds, no explosive tides. We never discussed her condition and its effects on the rest of us. It's as if we were all just holding our breaths until her diminished self could finally catch up with the rest of her that had ascended unscathed during the surgery.

Daddy Ben continued to take Poco to the country club on Friday nights. They continued to share a bedroom in their West University home. My grandfather took on the heavy load. Momma immediately jumped in to help. Daddy Ben kept Poco at home with him as long as he could, bringing in more and more help as her condition declined. He and my mom grew angel wings that first year after the surgery.

After the initial shock of my grandmother's surgery, we all shifted into a new routine. Every Thursday, my mother would bring Poco to our house to give her dad and the hired caretaker a day off. Poco would arrive dressed in a shirtwaist, nylon stockings covering her legs, sensible non-skid shoes on her feet. Her hair was always styled with a padded hairpiece in an ill-executed attempt to camouflage her sunken skull, a sheer hairnet securing its position. Holding onto her right elbow, Momma would escort Poco to her favorite spot on the den sofa next to the end table. An ashtray sat under the lamp, ready to hold the remnants of Poco's Pall Malls. The doctors told us she could still smoke, but not more than one cigarette an hour.

On Thursdays, when we got home from school, Robyn loved being the timekeeper for Poco's smoking schedule. Because Betsy wasn't as interested and I was too little, Robyn was in charge of doling out Poco's hourly cigarettes. She even got to strike the matches. Somebody would have to be there with her while Poco smoked to make sure she shook the ashes off before falling onto the couch or her clothing. The inevitable cigarette burns were eventually hidden under an arm cover.

Unable to carry on a normal conversation, Poco would sit in her favorite spot on the couch and, when not preoccupied with her smoking, repeat the same stories over and over again. "My mother died when I was born. They thought I had died too, laid me in the crook of my mother's arm. Saw me breathing. Used a dresser drawer for my crib, lined it with warm bricks."

The story would always come to a pause with her asking for another cigarette—"Is it time yet?" This would seamlessly transition into the children's finger play, "Here's the church and here's the steeple, open the door and there's all the people," lacing her fingers together, the two pointers left standing straight and tall to illustrate the rising spire. The finger play, as with the story about her birth, would be interrupted intermittently with another "Is it time yet?" And then the whole thing would start all over again—"My mother died when I was born...put me in a dresser drawer...here's the steeple..." And that was how she spent her day.

When Poco and Daddy Ben came to our house for dinner, which was often (we only lived ten minutes apart), my mom tied a cup towel around Poco's neck to catch the bits of corn or spinach, ground beef, or chocolate pudding that fell from her mouth. We all acted as if nothing unusual was happening, continued to talk about what we learned at school that day or how much tomatoes were costing this week at Kroger, comparing them to the prices at Weingarten's. When Poco choked and coughed, spewing the contents of her mouth onto the tablecloth, the conversation wouldn't skip a beat. "Friday, they were on for twenty-five cents a pound... I sat with Sammy and Cathy today at lunch. Cathy gave me a sip of her Cherry Coke... Hey Momma, can Susan come home from church with me on Sunday?" There was never a word of disgust, no wincing. We all got good at this game of charades, at ignoring this blatantly visible family secret to protect our grandfather's feelings—and, more importantly, our mother's. None of us wanted to do anything to cause her more pain, so we all unconsciously agreed to live in frozen grief.

Besides changing our outward familiar roles and family structure, an indelible emotional shift registered deep inside. Something morphed inside Daddy that was tangible, something intense and heavy with responsibility. Although he continued to whistle his Daddy-tune as he walked through the door after work each evening, he no longer scooped up his "Nancer" with delight. Somehow that precious pocket of "we-ness" that had kept us so close got lost in the shuffle. Perhaps Daddy was just stressed; perhaps coming home had become harder for him emotionally—I'll never know all of it for sure. What I do know is that I internalized that heart-wrenching loss. And because of that loss, on a deep, unconscious level, I decided he must not love me, not like he loved Betsy and Robyn. In my preschool mind, I assumed I must not be deserving of his love and etched that assumption into stone. I then buried it deep inside and held it tightly as a sacred truth.

As for my mother, her whole world was torn apart. Her heart was ripped to shreds. Though viscerally palpable, her grief remained unspoken. I have the body memory of her rocking me in our creaky, antique rocker, holding me tight like a little rag doll, sobbing her heart out, her pain infiltrating my body, the two of us aching as one. My mama was sad and brave and loving. I would be good and let her hold me close. I would be good and quiet because she needed me to be. Maybe if I sat really still and quiet, Mama would not be so sad; maybe some of the pain would melt away, and we could rock our way back to peace again.

But the rocking didn't take us anywhere. We just kept moving in place, back and forth, back and forth to the cadence of the creaking rocker. So, I stayed still and quiet and let my mother's broken heart beat inside my chest for as long as she needed it to.

Poco died when I was a freshman in college, some sixteen years after her original surgery.

The Seeping Ether

The other fault line that ran through our family did not barrel in like a tsunami. It was far more insidious. It penetrated every aspect of our lives like a virus injecting its genetic code into a permeable cell to replicate itself. This fault line was the fundamentalist church that we attended three times a week. *The Church*, as we referred to it, believing we were the only true believers destined for Heaven, was both the center and circumference of our world. Daddy's maternal grandfather was the fourth in a generational line of country preachers. His mother carried that lineage to her three sons. And, more than his two brothers, I think Daddy let it sink in the deepest.

By the time I was five and a half, all of the magic of innocence had evaporated out of our family and everything got really serious. In the summer of 1955, we moved from our home across the street from the swimming pool to the suburbs on the outskirts of town. We were so far out that rice paddies stretched across the horizon behind our house. At that same time, Daddy, after passing the Bar exam, opened a private law practice in downtown Houston. He also accepted a commission along with a handful of other young elders from our centrally located congregation to start a new satellite church in the suburbs. Those two new commitments, along with the shock waves that continued to reverberate after my grandmother's surgery, shook our family out of its idyllic daze into unconscious coping.

In her heartache after Poco's surgery, my mother split her dedicated attention between her daughters and her mother. My dad split his time and focus between developing his new law practice and starting a brand-new church. Looking back on it now, I can see how the constancy of our church-going and the church community that surrounded us provided much-needed stability. Our church family gave us a safe cocoon to nestle into. It gave us direction, a purpose, an identity we could count on. And for that, I will always be grateful. The community provided an extended family while its doctrines kept life simple. You didn't have to think for yourself. All the answers were provided for you. One less thing to worry about.

But *The Church* provided much more than simple stability. I made, and still have, many lifelong friendships with folks who share my fundamentalist roots. Those friendships run deep. Our common history, with all of its crazy quirks, its suffocating limitations, as well as its rays of light are intimately understood. That creates a heartfelt bond that newer friends just can't quite understand.

Although I admit that much of what I was taught required sifting later, being raised in *The Church* taught me, from the very beginning, that there is Something More to this life than what meets the eye. There is more here than a list of prerequisites for entering Heaven. There is more to life. I took this message in on a cellular level before I could cognitively understand it.

Paul Easley, the first preacher at our new church, preached his sermons through his heart. I couldn't understand the words he was using, but I could feel the depth of his inner knowing as tears streamed down his face. Brother Paul Easley, as we called him, spoke from somewhere inside himself that was deep and true and sure of love. At age six, I felt that. And that experiential proclamation of the benevolence of life has never left me.

There was one other preacher who stood out through all the years I spent in *The Church*: Ray Chester. Ray was the minister of the congregation we attended in Austin when I began to have children of my own. Ray was a philosopher. Ray was smart. Ray was a poet. Unlike the majority of the other preachers I experienced, Ray encouraged us to think for ourselves and to ask the tough questions. Ironically, it was that thinking and questioning that led me to leave *The Church* itself. It's an understatement to say that Ray played his part for me. He held me tight within the fold, and then like a good parent nudged me to fly on wings of my own.

Although my definition and experience with whatever that Something More is has morphed exponentially over time, I am ever so grateful that the idea of it was painted into my original mural.

But that was not all. My church experience was not limited to a sense of stability, lasting friendships, and an appreciation for Something More. It also exhaled virulent vapors as pervasive as the scent of my mother's cooking. The "God" from my fundamentalist upbringing had very specific but diametrically opposing characteristics that split him right in two—but not completely. He was still one God, but one who spoke out of both sides of his mouth. There was the God of love who exuded warmth and security, forgiveness and grace, who had the superpower ability to fill in all the holes in our very Swiss-cheesy human lives. Living with this half of God was like living under the spell of Cinderella's Fairy Godmother, who waved her magic wand and made everything all better again. This half of God made us feel all warm and gooey and safe inside.

The other half of God was scary and punitive, like being backed up against the wall by the Great Santini (see Pat Conroy, 2002), a punishment-driven father hell-bent on terrorizing his children into submission. That half of God had nothing to do with warmth and security. That half was downright petrifying.

Growing up in *The Church*, my sisters and I lived smack-dab in the middle of a perfect schizophrenic double-bind: we were taught to worship a God forever split by two equal but irreconcilable ways of relating.

Being a "good Christian," which of course is what we all wanted to be, meant striving for perfection, doing whatever it took to appease the Santini God. It meant always being on the lookout for how you had sinned and then right away praying for forgiveness to the Fairy-Godmother-God before you went to sleep at night, lest you die in an unforgiven state (and we all knew what that meant). This pressure was a constant.

Growing up, I lived in a downy-feathered, thorn-laced nest held together on all sides by fear, guilt, and shame. As crazy as this sounds, those three states of being were the hallmarks of what it meant to be a good Christian. What is so eye-popping, looking back on it now, is that living that way felt normal to us at the time. It was just the way of things. We didn't think to reflect upon it. We just accepted it as the gospel truth. My **Maggie-self**, who was the only self I knew myself to be at that time in my life, simply *trusted and obeyed* without the slightest question.

As a young person, this accepted way of life created a litany of challenges and conflicts. For example, my grandparents on my mother's side were Methodist and our aunt on our father's side was Presbyterian. They had all been christened as children but had not been immersed as adults, which, according to our tradition, was a mandatory prerequisite for entering through the gates of Heaven. Lying in the dark at night, right after my personal prayer for forgiveness and before drifting off to sleep, my innocent little heart would beg with the earnestness of pleading for a pony for Christmas, "Dear God, please, please, please don't let Poco and Daddy Ben and Aunt Helen go to hell. They're really good people. Please save them even though they haven't been baptized."

Of course, my **Maggie-self** was convinced that this was their only salvation because that is precisely what she had been taught. At the end of every sermon on Sunday mornings, at the Sunday evening worship service, and the closing of the Wednesday night Bible Study, the preacher would extend an invitation. The preacher would invite, encourage, and finally implore those who needed prayers or, more importantly, had not yet been baptized to come forward during the singing of the invitational song.

"Brothers and sisters, won't you come, as we stand and sing?" the preacher would begin as we opened our hymnals and raised our a cappella voices. "Let this be the day that you make your way down the aisle."

Almost persuaded now to believe.
Almost persuaded Christ to receive.
Seems now some soul will say, "Go Spirit, go Thy way;
Some more convenient day on Thee I'll call..."

We sang in concert to the preacher's beckoning as he made his way out of the pulpit and into the front of the sanctuary. "You know who you are," he would admonish over our hushed refrain as if the whole production had been choreographed ahead of time.

Almost persuaded, come, come today;
Almost persuaded, turn not away...
O wanderer, come...

"If you have need of prayer or if you have not yet confessed your faith in Christ and have not yet been cleansed by his blood, won't you come forward before it is too late as your brothers and sisters encourage you still?"

Almost cannot avail.
Almost is but to fail!
Sad, sad that bitter wail.
Almost, but lost!

Three times a week, not counting the nightly bedtime petitions, I hoped and prayed with all my might that this would be the day that my Aunt Helen, who remained a Presbyterian but who attended our church with her husband, my Uncle Clyde, would come forward and finally be immersed into the death and burial of our Lord and Savior. This brave act would override her infant christening, which we all knew didn't count anyway and was dooming her to spend eternity with the devil. Once we were all grown and beginning to come out of our childhood stupor, my sisters and I each confessed that we had privately prayed in earnest on behalf of the damned souls of our relatives. We all felt responsible for them.

The toxicity of our church remained unconscious throughout all of my growing-up years. It wasn't discussed until long after my sisters and I left home. Just like we didn't talk about our grandmother's condition, we never talked about the incessant fears and pressures, the conflicting messages that came along with our bone-rattling, knee-knocking indoctrination.

Although all three of us secretly prayed for Daddy Ben, Poco, and Aunt Helen to get themselves saved, that day never came. And God certainly never intervened. Having to live with that kind of dissonance and pressure as a child was excruciating. We lived with that pain incessantly gnawing at our insides like an intestinal bug. We *lived* with the pain, but we thought it was normal. It just came with the territory. We didn't make up the rules, and there was no thought of questioning their veracity. Even more so than with my lifelong friends from *The Church*, these shared experiences created a bond between my sisters and me that could never be broken. Of all the people on the planet, we three are the only ones who know in our cells and in our bones the constrictions, as well as the genuine love, the very real humanity that we were raised in.

It was *The Church's* unwavering literal interpretation of the Bible that made life so suffocating and its perimeter so very, very small. In that mindset, there was no room for a margin of error. When I was in high school, I went to a Christian camp for a week up near Mexia, Texas. This is in a very rural, northeast section of the state where words are spoken through the nose and drawn out slow and easy. Not only was the dialect different, but the mindset was different as well. I was from Houston, a big, metropolitan city, and although I was ensconced within a conservative denomination, it didn't compare to the legalism of our more small-town brothers and sisters.

On one particular evening, a visiting preacher from a nearby church came and delivered a rattle-your-bones, quake-under-the-big-Texas-skies, scare-the-hell-out-of-you Bible-Belt sermon. I realize now that the whole purpose of that Christian camp was focused on saving the souls of those teenagers who had not yet been baptized. It was an ordained mission.

On Sundays and every weeknight, visiting preachers from nearby towns would come in to offer the sermon. As was customary, the camp preacher offered an imploring invitation at the end of his sermon for anyone who wanted to be prayed for, who needed to ask for forgiveness, or—and we all knew this was the primary focus—who had not yet been baptized, to come forward as we sang the invitation song.

On that memorable evening, hordes of guilt-ridden teenagers moved by the fearmongering words of the preacher came forward in response to the invitation—most of them to confess some sin and to ask for forgiveness. There were three boys, however, who wanted to be baptized. Clearly, these kids had not been raised in *The Church* because those of us who had knew that if you weren't baptized by the time you turned thirteen, you were living on borrowed time.

After the sermon, the campers, staff, and the visiting preacher all walked down to the banks of the Navasota River to witness the three boys' salvation. After they confessed their faith, the first two boys were immersed without a glitch, but the third hit a snag. As the preacher lowered him back into the water, the kid's left hand rose into the air. We all saw it. I had never witnessed a *partial* before, and neither had anyone else. When the teenager was brought back up out of the water, the attending church fathers approached the preacher and told him what they had witnessed. They gathered in a little circle to discuss it, while the rest of us held our breaths. After a few minutes, a decision was made. "Better redo it, just to be safe." So, the immersion was repeated. Because, of course, we all knew "Almost...would not prevail."

At sixteen, this whole bizarre scene was confusing. A part of me recognized the ridiculousness of this kind of literal thinking, but at that time in my life questioning the authority was out of the question. I was still too entrenched within the cocoon that held me tight to let my confusion take me to anyplace new. So, I filed the whole thing away in a secret folder that I wouldn't open again for twelve more years.

* * *

If anyone at the time had suggested that our obsessive connection to *The Church* was a coping mechanism, we would first have been offended and then have flatly denied it. *The Church*'s perspective on reality *was* reality. We didn't see it as a *perspective*; we saw and claimed it as the truth, which is always how worldviews are experienced. More often than not, we don't see ourselves as surrounded and thus contained within a hand-painted illustration of reality. We just look out and believe that what we see is what is there. We don't realize that what we are looking at is a *picture* of reality, only as substantial as the **Canvas** it is painted on. For me, this recognition did not come until many, many years later.

The Christianity that I ingested right along with my mother's Southern cooking did not set me free as the Gospel proclaims. It instead held me captive in a very, very small, dark room like the lifeless gray **Foyer** in *The Great Artist's Dream*. And although I certainly do not live there like I did as a child, even at this late stage of my life that room still holds a scary, confined place inside my psyche. The three **Hungry Ghosts**—the little bald **Bookkeeper** relentlessly clacking away on his calculator, and his two insidious sidekicks, the **Preacher** and the **Protector**—still stand forever as gate-keepers at the entrance to the **Studio**. (Remember to refer to the Appendix to remember who these characters are.)

* * *

I know now that shattering life events start deep below the surface in a time before we have language when our bodies and our hearts, and **Souls** are busy taking notes. I know now that we imprint those notes into our personal archives and refer to them in every phase of our future lives. Life-shattering events are given meaning by everything that precedes them. And that is certainly true for my life. Each **Rupture** that I have experienced is inextricably tied to the blandness and conformity of the 1950s and to the awakenings of the 60s. It is linked to what I believed about being the baby of the family, the third daughter and sixth granddaughter, the last hope for a boy to carry the family name. It is tied to the deep sadness, the silence, and the newly adopted roles each of my family members took on in response to my grandmother's impairment, in my grandfather and mother's modeling of sacrificial love to the one in need. It is connected to my trying so hard to be good and still and quiet to protect my mother. It is certainly intertwined with everything I made up about my self-worth when Daddy's gaze turned away from me, his little "Nancer" running to meet him at the door, and toward the world of responsibility and my two older sisters who continued to capture his attention. All of the life-shattering moments in my life are anchored in how my family handled my grandmother's tragic injury. They are all woven into our collective blind adherence to the rigidity and encompassing cocoon of our family's fundamentalist church.

Life-shattering moments don't ever happen as isolated events. They are interwoven into the complex web of meaning that preceded them.

QUESTIONS FOR SELF-REFLECTION

1. Can you describe the most influential snapshots from your childhood? Did your family suffer any tragedies or ongoing trauma when you were growing up? If so, how did it affect you and your family as a system? If not, how would you describe your growing-up years?

2. Where are you in the birth order? How has that position affected your personality, your sense of self, how others relate to you? How does it differ from your siblings? If you are an only child, how has that affected your identity?

3. Which generation are you a part of—Baby Boomer, Generation X, Millennial, Gen Z? How has being born and raised in that era affected your identity and worldview?

4. What was your religious or spiritual upbringing during your growing-up years? Did you go to church/synagogue/mosque/other? Were you raised agnostic or atheist? How did that experience affect your worldview? How has it evolved?

5. What was the very best thing about your childhood? What are you most grateful for from those formative years? What have you had to discard along the way?

CHAPTER TWO
THE FATED DANCE

> *Romantic love delivers us into the passionate arms of someone who will ultimately trigger the same frustrations we had with our parents, but for the best possible reason! Doing so brings our childhood wounds to the surface so they can be healed.*
>
> - Harville Hendrix -

I met Josh, my former husband, on a church pew when we were just ten years old. His family had just recently moved to Houston. I had not yet entered the world of butterflies in the stomach or my heart skipping a beat over a guy, but even at that young age, the first time I saw Josh across the sanctuary, he caught my eye. I thought he was cute.

Over our pre-teen years, we became friends but didn't start dating until the summer between our junior and senior years in high school. That same summer of the unprecedented "partial" baptism in the Navasota River, Josh and I had our first kiss after he walked me back to my cabin. Although we went to our first two years of college at separate schools, Josh transferred to The University of Texas to be with me at the start of our junior year. We married in December of our senior year. I had turned twenty-one only one month before. We were babies but thought we were grown.

At our rehearsal dinner, the minister who performed the wedding ceremony made a toast—with iced tea, of course—that started with, "It's always been Josh and Nancy." Everybody in our tight little community thought of us as a couple. Our marriage was expected and celebrated. We were joining two first-tier families, making the whole circle tighter. We looked like a perfect fit, and in many ways we were.

We shared a common faith and heritage. We were both college-educated and eventually each went on to graduate school. We both wanted children and were family-oriented. We played and laughed easily with each other, but also had deep conversations about our goals in life and what we wanted for our future family. And besides all that commonality, we were madly in love. Over the years, our early childhood attraction morphed into a magnetic bond that was palpable. Unquestioned. Meant to be. By age nineteen, our fates were sealed. Together, like two pieces of a puzzle. (Refer to Michael Meade's quote at the beginning of Chapter One to distinguish between *fate* and *destiny*.)

As I reflect back on it, Josh and I were more like two magnetic sides of a zipper than two complementary puzzle pieces. Once our fates were brought together, we were both caught in the grips of the teeth of the thing—both of us feeling trapped and at the same time helpless to release the polarized pull of the magnet. We were what Harville Hendrix might call a perfect *Imago* match. According to this theory, our unconscious mind goes out looking for a partner that will be a perfect puzzle-piece-fit for our programmed self—my ***Maggie-self***. This partner does not resemble the perfect partner that our conscious mind is looking for, pencil in hand, desired characteristics listed on lined paper in order of priority. In fact, the *Imago* partner is the one who will trigger every part of our wounded self. In other words, however your partner shows up when he or she is threatened will be the very thing that threatens you the most. And vice-versa. The greater aim of the *Imago* match is not to torture us, although it feels that way at the time. Instead, it's life's way of providing us with the opportunity to choose to see the self and life differently—through the eyes of love instead of through the eyes of fear or lack. If we don't find our way to love and the original conflicting dynamic is left unconscious, the action-reaction-action-reaction dance-step goes around and around and around with no way out.

For many of us, it takes something earth-shattering for the gripper teeth to finally unzip. And that was certainly true for Josh and me.

After our honeymoon, we moved into a married-student apartment complex not far from campus. It was a second-floor studio with only one bedroom, a small study, a bathroom, a tiny living room furnished with Daddy Ben and Poco's hand-me-down white wicker furniture, and a kitchen only large enough for one of us to occupy at a time if the refrigerator door was open. Honestly, I could vacuum the whole thing without moving the plug. A four-by-four-foot railed deck overlooked the parking lot below. It was small but we were happy, at least at first, and we were on our own. We were playing out our prescribed roles and that felt good and safe and familiar.

Josh rode his bicycle to the McCombs School of Business where he got his MBA in record time. His hair was long and curled down his neck. Every day he wore his ragged blue jean cut-offs, his well-worn leather hiking boots, and some sort of T-shirt, sometimes collared and sometimes not. While Josh pedaled to school, I drove our little red stick-shift Valiant downtown to the Texas State Office of Early Childhood Development. I was originally hired on as a clerk, but within a few months worked my way up to Assistant to the Director of Parent and Public Education. I was the one bringing home the paycheck in those early days.

Josh graduated from the MBA program only one year after starting and immediately got a job through a recommendation from an old friend from church. The two guys who owned the company were a couple of well-connected high rollers in the world of Austin entrepreneurs. That first job launched Josh into a whole new universe. Made his head spin. He had never been around real movers and shakers before and he liked it.

I, on the other hand, felt like Josh was turning into a stranger. My bike-riding hippie had morphed into a suit-and-tie business mogul. His fascination with reading about the revolutionary dynamics of a coup d'état or the genius of Michelangelo was supplemented by reading *The Wall Street Journal*. He became a traditional conservative and started drinking Scotch and water in the evenings.

When I look back on it now, it seems to me that Josh's transformation from what I assumed to be an open-minded liberal (I think this was a fantasy on my part rather than the truth) to a ladder-climbing conservative did not create our differences. Rather, it exposed them. It happened early on, within the first two years of our marriage, and doggedly continued for another nineteen. That shift in Josh's identity and life-focus exposed what, from my perspective, was both his fated and destined drive to make the world his oyster.

From my vantage point, I can only assume that Josh's drive for increasing expansion, to claim more and more of life for himself, was fated from his role as the first-born son in the family, as the oldest and the biggest, as the one who started selling eggs to the neighbors when he was twelve and was throwing newspapers by age fourteen. Fated because his mother became pregnant again when he was only four months old, forcing him to grow up way too fast. His days of being the new baby were stolen from him before he cut his first tooth. I can only assume that Josh's position in the family put extra pressure on him to achieve, perform, excel, and to own a level of responsibility that was not expected of his younger siblings.

Yet Josh was not just *fated* to expand out into the world and claim it as his own. I believe that he was also *destined* from the very beginning to live large, to naturally take in the abundance that life has to offer, to be a leader, to take charge, to be smart and creative, and to know how to charm with a smile that brings sunlight into the room. I believe his destiny to live large was encoded into his *Soul* before any of his childhood programming ever took place. I know I couldn't possibly know all the ins and outs of Josh's drive to claim that oyster for his own. I can only piece it together from what I experienced in relation to him.

While Josh was busy making the world his oyster, by contrast, it was both my *fated* and *destined* drive to find the hidden pearl within it. From the moment Josh was launched into the world of entrepreneurship, his drive for more became insatiable. I matched every step of his spiraling outward by moving deeper and further inside myself. Given all the influences from my childhood, as the youngest-lost-child trying so hard to be good and still and quiet, I was fated to hide, to hold back, to assume that I didn't have the right to my unique place on the planet, to let others have their way. So, I played small while Josh played it out big. But I believe that I, like Josh, was also destined to intuitively move inside the self, to feel comfortable there, eager to learn its language and rhythm, to organically search for the hidden treasure.

This dynamic seemed to work for both of us, at least for a while. I didn't want to be in the limelight. I liked hiding in his shadow, and he liked being out there, big and bright. For a while, we found this a compatible arrangement, as did so many from our generation. This programmed dynamic allowed for both of us to play out our fated unfolding, which at that time in our lives was all we knew.

As could be predicted, however, the gap between us grew wider and wider. To exacerbate our division, Josh's job with the movers and shakers started to require him to travel, eventually up to fifty percent of the time. With this added responsibility, Josh began to make a lot of money. Making money became a new place for Josh's growing appetite, while I felt torn about it. I appreciated the money, his generosity in using it on behalf of the family, the security, and the added perks, but at the same time, I felt awkward. I didn't identify myself as wealthy. It embarrassed me and made me feel self-conscious. I felt out of place in that thin air while Josh thrived in it.

As Josh's world and worldliness expanded, I felt more and more left behind, insignificant, taken for granted, more like a placeholder or a steady anchor than a cherished partner. When I complained, cried, or screamed about this, Josh responded with anger, undoubtedly feeling criticized and taken for granted, in his own way. I felt shut down and extraneous. He must have felt attacked and held back. Neither of us felt appreciated. And that's where we would get stuck over and over again, having no idea where to go from there.

As humiliating as it is to admit, that's how we spent the next twenty years spinning around and around and around again—going nowhere. This was deeply painful and exhausting for both of us. I lived on amber alert with a constant knot in my stomach. Josh lived in an adrenaline rush running from the knot in his. Despite the expanding gulf between us, Josh and I maintained our mutual love of family and over six years had three children of our own: a daughter followed by two sons, whom we both adored and still do. They became the primary focus of our connection, while also maintaining close ties to both of our families and a group of close friends. Amidst moments of genuine connection and happy times, the tension was always there lurking in the background. For the most part, we kept the friction hidden. We loved looking like the perfect couple. It reinforced the charade and made it easier to keep it going. Neither of us wanted our dysfunction out in the public eye. After all, I had been trained from early childhood to hold a family image discreetly in place.

Ironically, when the kids were around five, nine, and

eleven years old, we had a family portrait made of the five of us walking hand-in-hand across a bluebonnet-covered hill, the wind blowing through our hair, big smiles across our faces. The photographer hung the picture in our local family diner as a marketing tool for her business where it remained for years to come. She would never know how closely she had captured our family—family image, that is. Funny. That portrait hung there on the wall, frozen in time even long after the divorce was signed and sealed.

While Josh was venturing further and further out into the big, wide world, I was holding down the home front with the kids while also attending graduate school. I started working on my master's in Human Growth and Development, taking just one class a semester while the kids were still little. That decision opened up a whole new set of rooms in my psyche. This was one of my first moves into the *Studio*—one of the first times I dared to paint an image of my very own on my *Collage*. Going back to school was a choice I made by me and for me. And with that decision, I discovered a big, wide world of my own, but my big, wide world was interior. It led me deep into the world of psychology and spirituality, which extended from the classroom outward into my personal life.

During our late twenties, Josh and I drifted away from *The Church* of our childhood. We reached a point where we no longer felt in sync with its rigid literalism, and so we left it to explore other beliefs and practices. While I don't consider this movement a *Rupture*, it did require me to take important steps as depicted in the *Dream*: to walk into the *Studio*; to walk past the judgmental glares of the *Hungry Ghosts*; to eventually tire of the humdrum paintings *Maggie* liked to replicate; and to begin to paint new, unknown images on the *Canvas* that only *Nancy* could imagine. Though this movement was difficult, it wasn't heart-wrenching. It felt like an organic welcomed emergence. And although Josh and I left *The Church* together, moving away undoubtedly carried a unique meaning for each of us.

Within our marriage, both Josh and I began to live a double life. Mine was at home with the kids and at the university with my books. Josh's was on American Airlines and at the Park Plaza Hotel in New York City. Our individual pursuits were deeply satisfying to both of us, as our relationship with each other became more and more polarized. Over time, Josh became bored with my colorless home life and had little appreciation for my internal adventures. He began to demand more and more that I match his extroverted, exuberant lust for life. But, try as I might, there was no way I could keep up with him. Josh kept saying he was looking for *spectacular*. I never quite knew what that meant but felt pretty certain that I didn't want it, at least not his version of it.

We went to marriage counseling off and on, but nothing ever helped. The truth is that neither of us was ready to face the truth about ourselves or our marriage. During each visit, we'd spend the entire fifty-minute session blaming the other with bulleted lists of complaints to validate our opposing points of view. We both thought if the other could change, we would be okay. This is a very common mistake that leads to nowhere. It just keeps the dance in place. We honestly didn't know any better.

Although we both felt tortured, we couldn't see any other options. This is the strength of denial. This all sounds so stupid now, but we were simply living out our childhood programming, which at that time in our lives was all we knew. Neither of us wanted to get a divorce. The very thought of it terrified us—the guilt, the shame, the failure of it all, the fear of what it would do to our children. Neither of us knew how to live independently without the other. We had co-created a symbiotic identity that had frozen in place. Staying stuck was deadening. Moving out was terrifying. A true Catch-22.

Thank God, the pressure to keep this charade together finally took us to a point of no return. During the Christmas holidays of 1993, Josh and I took the kids skiing in Taos, New

Mexico. As fate would have it, this turned out to be the vacation from hell. To start with, the late-night drive from the airport to the cabin we had rented in the mountains was grueling. The streets leading out of the airport had been cleared and were easily passable, but the country road that led to the cabin was covered in a thick layer of solid ice. Our rental car came equipped with snow chains, but because you can't drive on clear roads with them on, they were stored in the trunk. As soon as Josh turned onto the first ice-covered road, the car started to slip and slide. This meant he had to get out into the dark, freezing night air and put the chains on while I carefully inched the car forward each time he got one in place. The kids' job was to stay still and quiet inside the car.

So there we were, in the pitch-dark and frigid New Mexico mountains in the last week of December. Josh pulled the car as far off the road as possible, got the chains out, and started the arduous task of linking them together, one tire at a time. He was irritated, cold, and frustrated. His frustration turned to anger and then to blaming and cursing.

I couldn't blame Josh for being frustrated or even getting angry at the situation. I don't know anyone who could have maintained their composure under those circumstances, but the energy that he emitted in the face of it felt pointed at us. It felt just like the Great Santini God all over again. We all felt his resentment as if he were sorry he had come at all. Things had suddenly turned very tense, which is how they stayed for the rest of the trip.

Yes, we skied during the day, got hot chocolate in the warming house in the afternoons, and ate dinner every night in the cabin by a roaring fire, but underneath the happy-family vacation facade, the pressure cooker was about to explode.

The second-to-last night of the trip happened to be our twenty-first wedding anniversary. After the kids went to bed, Josh was expecting a romantic celebration. I was not up for it. Not by a long shot. Josh had been in a state of irritation, his anger lurking right under the surface or fully exposed ever since the tire ordeal. When he wasn't angry, he was preoccupied. All semblance of relatedness had long since walked out the door. The last thing I felt for him on that anniversary night was any kind of closeness, much less anything to celebrate. I could feel something inside of me inviting me to move out of my fear. As scary as it was, I once again accepted *The Great Artist*'s invitation and made another move into the *Studio*. I stood my ground and told Josh no, I was not interested in his advances. I wasn't going to live according to his idea of what my truth should be. I was going to act from my own experience of my own truth.

And that did it. Josh erupted. "I can't believe you!"

We so didn't want the kids to hear us through the split-pine walls, so Josh shouted at me in whispered tones, "You won't have sex tonight?! Tonight?! It's our anniversary! Nancy! It's our anniversary!"

Muffling my response but expressing with equal passion, I made my position clear. "I don't feel close to you, Josh! I don't feel like celebrating! I can't do it! I can't do it! Don't you get it? I can't!"

It might seem that this fight was about differences in libido or maybe it was just a power struggle. Maybe it was about the use of intimidation or passive-aggression, two equal forms of manipulation. On one level, all of these relational dynamics were at play. But they do not come close to capturing what the fight was really about. No, that struggle was a come-to-Jesus moment between denial and consciousness, between illusion and truth, between fate and destiny.

During those tumultuous years of our lives, Josh and I were both caught inside our own collective murals on the back wall of our private *Studios*. We had become nothing more than painted characters on a *Canvas*, held in place by the insidious shame-tauntings and fear-tactics of the *Hungry Ghosts* who had followed us in from the *Foyer*.

*Clackity-clackity-clack...the sound of the **Bookkeeper's** keys filtering throughout the background...*

For one pristine moment on our twenty-first anniversary, I dared to step outside my programmed identity by telling Josh no and holding my ground. This thrust me into a new and terrifying reality. With my declarative "No" and Josh's reaction to it, we were inching our way to the top of a very steep pinnacle. We had no idea we were headed for free fall.

QUESTIONS FOR SELF-REFLECTION

1. Can you identify with living in a state of denial—either about a relationship that on some level you knew was not authentic or in some other realm of your life (an addiction, for example)? What are ways that you have compromised yourself because you were too afraid to fully own the truth?

2. Because each one of us carries our own unique set of DNA and our own unique set of circumstances during our childhoods, each of us will have a unique programmed or fated self. I call mine *Maggie*. That is the part of me that absorbed all that was going on in my family when I was growing up. She learned to be good and still and quiet, to conform to what was expected of her. My *Maggie-self* is a rule-follower. She does not think on her own. She is not adventurous. She lives out of fear, guilt, and shame. In *Dream* terms, *Maggie* is always under the authority of what I call my *Hungry Ghosts*—the *Bookkeeper* who keeps a constant tally of *Maggie's* behavior, the *Preacher* who constantly demands that she be perfect, and the *Protector* who forever scares her into playing it safe. Your fated self may be very different from mine. Can you identify the characteristics of your *Maggie-self*? The characteristics of your inner childhood authorities? What are they? What would you name them? Can you see how and why you took on those characteristics? Can you see how these aspects of the self always work in tandem? In what ways do you still live out of that fated identity?

3. Can you see how I carried some of the assumptions that I adopted as truth when I was a child into my adulthood? Into my marriage? If you go up high and look down on the timeline of your own life, can you see the direct links between your childhood assumptions and who you are as an adult? If you are married, can you connect any of your childhood assumptions to the dynamic that you currently have with your spouse or have had in past relationships?

4. What are some examples from your own life when you consciously moved out of your *Foyer* and into your *Studio*—when you consciously moved out of your fate and into your destiny like I did when I refused to have sex with Josh on our anniversary? In other words, can you point to a moment in your life when you acted solely on your own, outside the bounds of your childhood programming? If so, what prompted that kind of independent thinking and action?

CHAPTER THREE
I DIED. I LIVE.

*Denial is the shock absorber for the soul.
It protects us until we are equipped
to cope with reality.*

- C. S. Lewis -

A few weeks after we got home from our Taos trip, our therapist and leader of our *A Course in Miracles* discussion group, Dr. Frank Allen, announced that he was offering a five-day retreat in March called a Spirit Quest. I know now this was another invitation from **The Great Artist** to move into the **Studio**. I accepted his invitation again and immediately signed up for the retreat. I didn't know what a Spirit Quest might entail, but it didn't matter. I needed to stop. I needed to stand still and get a hold of myself. I was aching for something far bigger and wiser to help me. I was desperate. Josh agreed to stay in town to keep the kids on his own for the five days I would be gone. Although this was not conscious at the time, I would no longer live entirely as **Maggie** in the **Foyer**. A new space was beginning to open up inside of me.

At the retreat, each participant was given the opportunity to do his or her own personal work surrounded by the support of the other group members. On the fourth day of the retreat, it was my turn to sit in the hot seat.

"No more! No more! No more!" I screamed at the top of my lungs, striking the Gestalt chair with a pillow.

"Nancy, what is it that you want?" Frank asked me. The other retreat participants sat silently in a circle around me.

I thought for a moment. Good question. What was it that I wanted?

"I want to be heard. I want to be listened to. I want to be respected. I want my thoughts and feelings to carry as much weight as everybody else's." I said this sort of matter-of-factly. I realize now that I wasn't fully inhabiting my own body, but I didn't know it at the time. I was there, yet not there all at once. Dissociation felt normal to me.

Frank leaned forward, looked me straight in the eye, and asked again, "Nancy, what is it that you want?"

As I listened to his repeated question, I felt a familiar clench in my stomach, a sensation that felt like a very old friend. My breathing was hard and rhythmic. I reached further inside myself and sat silent for a minute, reaching down deep. It was like trying to catch a drifting cloud or the tail of some elusive creature that kept slipping out of reach. I stayed with it, concentrating hard. It came to me as a startling discovery: *clarity.* Inside, I suddenly felt clear.

I leaned forward in my chair, matching Frank's stance, placed my hands on my knees, and looked him straight in the eye. "I want to be reckoned with," I said. It was as if all of the molecules in my body coalesced and joined forces. I felt a solidity in my core that I had never felt before.

"Now you're getting there," he said. And then asked one more time: "Nancy, what is it that you want?"

What is up with him?! I wondered. Why does he keep asking me this same question?

I scrambled inside, sitting quietly, trusting that if he kept asking, there must be more to the answer. I returned to my earnest concentration. Then, boom! I raised my hands above my head and shouted, "I want a birthday!"

"Turn on the music! Everybody, get up and dance. This is Nancy's birthday! Let's help her celebrate."

Everyone in the room jumped to their feet as Kool & The Gang's "Celebration" came over the loudspeakers. The words and beat of the music filled the room with an energetic aliveness. After the intensity of the day, we were all swept up into joyful intoxication. Laughter, skipping, twirling, clapping hands, and jive-moves reverberated through the air, catching us all up into a growing sense of oneness. We began to travel around the room in unison like a murmuration of starlings that suddenly swoops and dives as one, yet not consciously understanding why or how. Something in me had opened up wide for the first time and stretched into brand-new territory like a chick peeking through a tiny crack in its incubating eggshell, exposing a glimpse of the big wide world outside—exciting and terrifying all at the same time. My destiny was beginning to break through my denial.

Little did I know what that moment of clarity had set into motion. But I will be forever grateful to it for giving me the taste of freedom I needed to keep moving forward.

That electrifying moment of clarity in the Spirit Quest turned out to be truly the tiniest tip of the iceberg. I hadn't traveled nearly as far as I thought I had. A part of me, my *Nancy-self*, was steadily stepping out of my *Maggie-self*. I was living more of my life in the *Studio*, but it would take years for this to become fully conscious. Developing a stronger sense of self is not a one-and-done kind of deal.

The Friday I got home from the Spirit Quest, and after we spent some time with the kids, I confronted Josh with my newfound resolve. I told him that I was determined to get to the bottom of our marriage. I wanted to know the truth, to put all the cards out on the table and turn them over one by one. I wanted us to flat-out tell the truth about what we both felt and thought. I wanted to get to the bottom of our list of "favorite" arguments—money, sex, power, alcohol, his flirtations with other women, his intimidation, my hiding, his lying, my criticism, my giving him just enough to keep him temporarily satisfied, no more and no less. "Let's get it all out, once and for all."

I told him I was going to get to the truth either way, with him or without him. My preference was for him to join me, but I would peel off the layers by myself if he didn't choose to come on board. This was my *Nancy-self* standing full-blown in the *Studio*. Josh could feel the shift in energy. In response to this declaration, he did something he had never done before. He got a piece of paper and a pen and said, "I want to write this down." Shockingly, he heard me and took me seriously. Then he declared, "I'm going to the lake house to think about this. I'll be back on Sunday and let you know what I have decided."

I followed him into our walk-in closet, stopped him from packing, and pulled him in close. We held each other tight, both of us starting to cry. Something in each of us knew that we were entering new territory without a map—one of those liminal places, neither here nor there. But there we were, standing in the closet holding each other, surrounded by our clothes. It was surreal, a mind-boggling juxtaposition. Behind me, my dresses, my broom-stick prairie skirts, my Osh-Kosh denim overalls hung high on a rod, a mishmash of color. Behind Josh, his suit jackets hung over their matching dress pants, a blur of dark gray and black and deep navy blue. His polished leather shoes sat in straight rows on the shoe rack next to us. The scent of *Sunflower*, my favorite cologne, and Josh's Kiwi shoe wax mingled together in the air.

It was all so familiar. Our clothes hung there like always, ignoring the rumbles of a deep, hidden turbulence. Our familiar fragrances filled the air just like they did every day. But nothing was the same. It was as if the world had suddenly turned on its axis. His suits, my long skirts, his leather dress shoes set so straight, my paint-splattered overalls. Those mingling intimate scents. It was all so commonplace. It was all so *us*. And yet from that moment on, nothing would ever be the same.

Josh drove out to spend the weekend at our lake house and came home on Sunday, as promised. I spent the weekend terrified that I had made an irrevocable mistake. What if I had gone too far? What if this was the end? What had I done? The *Hungry Ghosts* inside of me used every tactic they could to bring me deeper into self-doubt, but I didn't call Josh and beg him to come home. I didn't take anything back. I left him at the lake house and I stayed put, taking care of the kids in a daze and praying. I just prayed my ass off. My inner Voice kept reminding me to breathe, to trust. "Stay with it. Play this out. It's taking you somewhere. You are not alone. We are with you."

After Josh got home that Sunday afternoon, we spent time together as a family. After the kids went to bed, Josh circled back around and reported, "I thought a lot about what you said on Friday night. I journaled about it. And what I wrote was this —'I can fake it. I can leave it. Or, I can try to fix it... I choose to fix it.'"

The next day, we called Frank and booked him for the next weekend, the entire weekend. No more of this fifty-minutes-a-week business. We were ready to clear this thing out. At 10:00 the following Saturday morning, we sat once again in his office, like we had so many times before. But this time, we were earnest, ready to lift the veil. I started by confronting Josh. I let it all out about his drinking, his lying, his drive for money and power, and his use of intimidation with me and the kids. I confronted him head-on about his attraction to other women. I wasn't going to back down this time. I was going to stand in my truth. And I was asking for his. I told him, "Josh, I am not deaf, dumb, blind, stupid, or crazy, but I have acted as if I were. What's the truth, the real truth about you and other women?"

Josh was silent for a few minutes and then began to purge. He started telling me about a series of affairs he had had, the first one starting at a New Year's Eve costume party we had gone to at a neighbor's house in our mid-twenties. I remembered that party well. Most of us got carried away that night, taking on the persona of our costumed alter-egos—gypsy girls with tinkling bangles, black cats dressed in slinky spandex, the guys all cool with slicked back hair like the Fonz or Tony Manero from *Saturday Night Fever*. I remember feeling almost intoxicated by the pheromones that filled the room that night. It was easy to let down my guard. I wanted to let it down so I could finally step out of all of my childhood religious restrictions. I wanted to play with matches. I wanted to join the sexual revolution. And so, I did. Sort of. This was my ego-driven **Nancy-self** painting self-indulgent images on the **Canvas**. She was so tired of coloring inside the lines.

After that intoxicating night of breaking all the rules, Josh and I had a handful of encounters with two of the other couples from the party. We all agreed that we were permitting ourselves to stretch beyond the boundaries of our marriage vows, but within limits. We all agreed that we could play around but not take it all the way, so to speak. We felt safe experimenting with people that we knew while all being upfront about it. No sneaking around behind anybody's back. Or so we all assumed.

But I was naive.

After a few rounds of that heady ego-gratification, I couldn't handle it anymore. I felt all jumbled up inside. I felt sick—torn in half. Part of me loved the attention. I loved feeling desired. I loved breaking out of my legalistic straitjacket. I loved defying my inner **Hungry Ghosts** with their warnings and their shaming, acting out for the first time in my life—but living in that space began to feel dishonest. It wasn't who I wanted to be in the core of me, beyond just what the **Hungry Ghosts** expected.

I set up an appointment with a pastoral counselor to discuss the rule-bending Josh and I had been exploring. Spilled the beans in the first session. His response to me was, "I would never do anything like that." You can imagine what that did to me. I immediately retreated into shame. That therapist missed a golden opportunity to take me to a deeper, truer part of my identity but that didn't happen. On my own, however, something inside of me came to a full stop. I told Josh I couldn't play around like that anymore. We needed to bring the thing to a close. So, we met with the other couples and everyone agreed to stop it. There were no arguments. It never happened again.

But, again, I was naive.

In our couple's session, Josh confessed that on that fateful New Year's Eve night, he had stepped over the line, while the rest of us had just flirted with it. While the rest of us had played with matches, Josh had lit a bonfire. Once he stepped over that boundary, it got easier and easier for him to step over it again and again, especially because he never got caught. There were never any consequences. Although I suspected almost all of the women Josh had had affairs with, and although I confronted him with my suspicions every time, my willingness to back down in the face of his indignant reaction enabled him to keep it up. But I am jumping ahead with this recognition.

When I asked Josh to join me in a new level of honesty, I knew I had asked for the truth. I know now that in aligning myself with truth, my *Nancy-self* unconsciously aligned herself with my *Soul-self*. I hadn't ever done this before. I had never consciously chosen to live in truth like this, not this boldly. The truth is what I wanted, but I had no idea what it would feel like to hear it, what it would feel like to be bombarded by it.

Josh's confessions hit me to the core. My stomach clenched. My heart ached. I was catapulted into a very strange, conflicted place. A part of me felt relieved that my suspicions were finally being validated. A part of me felt grateful that Josh was finally telling the truth, but the emotional price for that validation was traumatizing. I had to face the fact that Josh and I had been living in an illusion of our own making. I had spent over two decades with a man who could look me in the eye and bald-faced lie to me, over and over again while I matched him every step of the way with my fear-based willingness to stay in denial by lying to myself.

After Josh's revelations, I sat there in Frank's office, dumbfounded, in a daze. The stark truth of it was too much for me to take in, not only about the other women but about me and the degree to which I had been sleepwalking. I wanted to know the truth, the whole truth, but its effect on me was more than I could bear.

I heard the rip as **The Great Artist** *sliced his X-ACTO knife down the side and across the bottom of the giant canvas. I looked up and felt the pain, the shock, the betrayal in that act of violation. A part of me screamed, "NOOO!" at the top of my lungs in disbelief.*

This first **Rupture** sliced right through the part of the **Canvas** that held **Maggie** and **Nancy** together as one. Although my **Nancy-self** had previously made some decisions that were by her and for her, none of those choices created such a huge rift between her identity and **Maggie**'s. Somehow those decisions—deciding to go to graduate school or even to leave *The Church* of my childhood, which took years—weren't so threatening to my **Maggie-self**. But to go along with this one would stretch **Maggie** further than she was willing to extend. She knew it would break her. So, she refused to go the distance. My **Maggie-self** wanted my **Nancy-self** to stop all this truth-telling so she could keep painting what she'd always known.

After Josh's round of confessions, we took a lunch break. I went home alone and walked around the empty house, moaning and sobbing, hurting all over. I was in shock. Everything I believed in had been ripped apart and exposed as a lie. It took me outside myself and my known reality. I was free-floating in a no-man's-land.

And this brings us full circle, back to that moment where my fate and my destiny collided. Would I choose to walk through the gaping hole in the **Canvas** or stay transfixed on the **Rupture**?

I crumpled down to the floor and scrunched myself into a fetal position next to the bed skirt of our king-sized bed. "I don't want you!" I screamed at God, tears streaming down my cheeks, snot running from my nose—I didn't care. A surge of anger, angst, terror, and desperation rose from my clenched stomach through my ruptured heart and out of my throat into convulsing sobs. "I don't want you!" I shouted again. Then the words were absorbed in my gasping, my inability to breathe, turning into that kind of crying where the pain pierces so deeply no sounds can emerge. I felt a wrenching stab that ran all the way through the core of my body. Through my sobbing, I managed to take a deep breath and shout again, "I don't want you! I want him!" But I knew I didn't have him, and I hadn't for a very long time.

"So, I'll take you," I finally said. "You're all I've got." And Spirit reached down, stretched out its hand, and simply said, "Happy Birthday, Nancy!"

QUESTIONS FOR SELF-REFLECTION

1. Have you ever acted out of pure ego gratification, when you deliberately broke a rule or "colored outside the lines" like I did at that fateful New Year's Eve party? What part of you was satisfied through that act of self-indulgence or defiance? How did you feel later?

2. Can you identify with both my *Maggie-self* and my *Nancy-self* during this stage in my life? How would you describe each of them? How would you characterize the differences between your *Maggie* and *Nancy* parts of yourself as they have played out in your life? Which one do you identify with most of the time? How have those two parts of yourself reacted in response to your *Canvas Ruptures*?

3. The intensity and the shock of my first *Rupture* tie directly back to some of the assumptions I adopted in my childhood, both from my religious upbringing and my family's dedication to keeping family business quiet. If you have experienced a *Rupture* in your own life, one that shredded your whole sense of self, can you tie the intensity of it back to the influences or experiences from your formative years? If you have not yet experienced a *Rupture*, what is your experience of reading about mine?

4. In the last chapter, I described the first moment that I realized I could no longer keep denying the validity of my own experience—that was when I refused to make love on my anniversary. In this chapter,

when Frank kept asking me, "Nancy, what do you want?" I experienced another layer of denial being peeled away. Have you ever experienced your own denial about something getting peeled off in layers? What was that like for you?

CHAPTER FOUR
FROM FATE TO DESTINY

*Set within the seed of the soul is not
just a fleeting image or a vague pattern
but a lifelong story enfolded within, waiting to be
cracked open and lived all the way out.*

- Michael Meade -

After that marathon therapy session, Josh and I agreed to separate. I called each member of my family and told them I needed help. I was falling apart. And they all came. All of them. My mother, my father, and my two older sisters came and stayed with me for the next ten days. I couldn't eat. I couldn't sleep. I couldn't take care of my children by myself. I lost thirteen pounds in three weeks. I had to take sleeping pills at night to get any semblance of rest. And then, little by little, one baby step at a time, I began to claim my new identity, the one built on truth. But truth be told, it was a hard transition.

After all that honesty permeated the room, Josh and I knew we needed a break. The agreement was that we would separate for the next three months, but continue to meet regularly for therapy. We also agreed that we would keep our marriage vows intact during that time and that if we no longer wanted to keep those vows in place, we would be honest and tell each other. He would live at the lake house, and the kids and I would live in our family home in town. They would visit him on the weekends. We would only talk when we needed to about our kids or at our planned therapy sessions.

Each of the kids had his or her reaction to the turmoil. We asked Frank how we should handle telling them about the reasons for our sudden separation, and he suggested that we keep it pretty generic, but to answer all direct questions honestly. Eventually, all three of them asked if their dad had been with other women. At different times, each had suspected it. We answered each one of them with respect, and honesty, and humility, trying to stay age-appropriate (Emmie, age sixteen; Cade, age fourteen; and Jack, age ten) with our responses, each of us owning as much personal responsibility for the mess we had co-created. We assured them that we both loved them dearly and that our differences had nothing to do with them. And then, we got all of them into therapy.

It may seem strange that I didn't up and divorce Josh at this point, but his willingness to finally tell me the truth made him feel trustworthy for the first time in a long time. We both wanted to see if we could forge a new relationship based on honesty, vulnerability, and ownership of responsibility after our separation.

* * *

Let me stop the storytelling here to put this decision in the context of the evolution of consciousness. On the *Front Side of the Canvas*, we are living our lives based on concepts and assumptions about who we are and what life is about. Following *The Great Artist* through a *Rupture in the Canvas* is a step into truth, a space beyond any conceptualization. For me, moving into greater alignment with truth meant claiming and then acting from a stronger sense of self. To move out of the *Foyer*, away from my allegiance to the *Hungry Ghosts* and into my *Soul-self*, I had to start claiming my unique space on the planet. I could no longer hide or live out of self-deprecation.

This isn't everyone's path through the **Canvas**, though. This movement toward a stronger sense of self is appropriate for those who, like me, grapple with questioning our worth. For folks whose **Hungry Ghosts** left them with an exaggerated sense of self, stepping through the **Canvas** requires releasing some degree of an exaggerated ego and recognizing the equal value of others. Both of these realignment processes use the shock of a **Rupture** to bring the self into a healthy balance with others.

Denial peels off in layers. Getting to a truly balanced perspective, seeing the dynamic clearly from a bird's-eye view, is a process. At first, as you might imagine, I felt very much victimized by Josh. I saw him as the villain in the relationship. It took a long time for me to see how our two puzzle pieces fit together perfectly. I now know you can't have one without the other, and that my denial and passive acceptance fueled his behavior, but the fullness of that realization would not come for many years.

* * *

Back to the story. As part of my continued healing, I asked Josh for the names and addresses of each of the women he had been with so I could write to each of them. I started my letter by asking its recipient to read it in its entirety, after which they could burn it or throw it away. I didn't care. I then introduced myself to them as Nancy, Josh's wife. I wanted them to know that I would no longer play the role of a phantom person living in the wings of his life. I was real. I had a name and a life of my own. I was the mother of Josh's three children. I was writing to tell them that whenever they visualized their times with Josh, to now see me and our three children standing at the foot of the bed, right there in the room with them. They could pretend that we didn't exist and that their rendezvous with Josh were private affairs, but in truth, their actions had and were still having deep effects on all of us. After they read the letter, they could do anything with that information they wanted. It was up to them. I addressed and stamped the envelopes and put them in the mail, trusting that the truth would take over from there.

In our therapy sessions during our separation, it really did feel like Josh and I were coming together. We were continuing to learn about ourselves and how we had each played a part in creating such a convoluted mess. Over those months, I believed that we were, to the best of our ability, trying to find our way back to each other, to remember the very real love that lived underneath our mistaken assumptions about ourselves, love, marriage, and truth. It seemed that we were on the road toward greater healing.

* * *

While we were creating this new bond, I was completing my doctorate in Developmental Psychology. These two major segments of my life had been following a parallel track.

Just before my doctoral graduation, I had an experience that exposed how these two equidistant lines in my life intersected. I will never really know its real significance, but I choose to believe that our Guides use everything on our behalf, anything that will catch our attention.

I asked my good friend, Sharon, to go with me to San Antonio to shop for a new outfit to wear to my graduation. I found some silk, flowy pants in muted pastels and a moss-green linen jacket. I was thrilled with the find. On the way home, Sharon and I decided to stop by a monastery, a mystical place that we had heard about for years. Yes, in hole-in-the-wall Blanco, Texas, no less! This was a Greek Orthodox convent located, of all places, on a hardscrabble goat farm. It was known for its myrrh-weeping Mother Mary icon. Folks came from all around to witness the tears and receive a blessing from the sacred Mother.

Sharon and I are not Greek Orthodox. We're not even Catholic. In fact, we had both been raised in the Bible Belt of the South. But as adults, we were also both fascinated with all things spiritual and esoteric and were open to experiencing the sacred in any of its forms. We didn't know if icons could cry tears of myrrh from some undefinable, sacred space or if the nuns squirted the tears on the image with an eyedropper after hours. And we didn't really care. We wanted to experience the place with curiosity and leave all judgment back in the hardscrabble pastures.

We drove up the winding gravel road, goats grazing behind wire fencing on either side until we got to a parking lot. We discovered several small buildings built in a semicircle. Hanging on one of them was a sign that read something like "*Mother Mary Icon Viewings*." We walked up to the door and opened it gently. An extremely tall—she must have been over six feet—Orthodox African American nun, dressed in full black habit from head to toe, came to the door to let us know that the session had just started but she would wait for us.

Noticing that we had come bare-headed and in casual summer attire, she showed us a cardboard box filled with a collection of crumpled, handmade wrap-around skirts and another filled with scarves and lace hankies. She instructed us to tie a skirt over our shorts and to put a scarf or handkerchief on our heads. Clearly, we had come unprepared.

Putting hand-sewn skirts over our shorts and lace doilies on our heads exposed the ridiculousness of this adventure. Looking at each other in this strange attire got us laughing. We were suddenly struck with the outlandishness of what we were doing. We had stepped so far out of character, but there was something about this stretching that enabled us to lay our cynical skepticism aside. Either we were going all out or we were going to stay within the bounds of rationality. We chose to trust in the beyond-the-pale of the moment, despite our very educated reservations.

After a few minutes, the nun came back out and escorted us into the tiny viewing room. The Mother Mary icon was placed reverently on a podium in the center of the space. An overhead spotlight lit her face with a golden glow. About four or five other women were already there standing quietly in a circle around the image. They were all dressed in their Sunday best with lace mantillas draped over their heads.

The nun escorted us to view the icon individually. She explained to each of us that Mary was not weeping that day, but showed us the stains left from previous tears, and then asked if we would like to be blessed by the Holy Mother. When it was my turn to view the image and accept the blessing or not, I said yes without hesitation. She asked me if I had a particular petition for the Mother, and I said, "Yes, I need final clarity about my marriage. I need a sign to tell me what to do."

The nun said a prayer to Mother Mary on my behalf, requesting a sign of clarity. I closed my eyes and moved into a genuine space of connection as she worded the prayer. I sank down deep inside myself into a place of quiet reverence. It was as if the others in the room had been blanketed from my awareness. In that one moment of petition, it was just me and the Holy Mother, the sacred archetype of all that is nurturing, comforting, the Divine Presence of outpouring love in compassion for the human condition. At that moment, it was just me and Mary and the earnestness of my prayer. I could not have articulated it at the time, but I had moved into that miraculous liminal space again where things are neither literal nor abstract, a place that my rational mind couldn't go with me, but a place that I was beginning to recognize and love. After her prayer, the nun drew the symbol of the cross on my forehead with her thumb. I returned to the circle with an open heart, ready to look for signs, trusting that they would come.

The following Friday night, Josh threw a surprise graduation party for me at the home of one of our friends. When we walked through the front door, all of my friends and family were lined up on the spiraling staircase in the foyer. They beamed back at me as they shouted, "Surprise!" in unison. Josh had done an incredible job orchestrating all of it and I was truly surprised. I felt taken aback by all the outpouring of love that flooded in my direction. Josh had put so much attention into every detail, knowing exactly what I would want. I felt my heart open to him again, despite the pain that he had caused me. The love and the pain always seemed to go together. I know now that this moment was a joyful quiet before the storm.

The next day, May 14, 1994, was the day of my graduation from my full-time, six-year doctoral program. To say that it was a milestone is to miss the real importance of the event. It wasn't just the completion of an academic goal—it marked the arrival of my coming out, my movement from fated bird in the cage to my destined flight out into the world, flying on my own fledgling wings.

Before I left for the ceremony, I went to check the mail and found two letters in the box addressed to me. One was from somewhere in the States—I can't remember which one, maybe California—and the other was from Australia. I opened them immediately and knew they were from two of the women I had written introducing myself. Unwittingly, they both revealed that Josh had been with them during the time of our separation, exposing that he had not stayed true to our agreements. He was still at it and still lying about it.

My body reacted to this revelation just like it had in those truth-telling sessions in Frank's office. My stomach knotted up. My heart raced and ached. My whole being hurt. I walked slowly into our bedroom where Josh was getting dressed and showed him the letters. What could he say? He was caught and our whole house of cards came tumbling down, once and for all.

My prayer had been answered. I was hit with the power and the rawness of undeniable clarity. Mother Mary had sent me an unequivocal sign. It took my breath away.

Somehow, I managed to get in my car and drive myself to the university. I stood in line just like all the other graduates and acted as if my life had not just lost all of its integrity. Josh and the kids came together in his car and sat in the stands. They watched as I walked up on stage in my black graduation gown, three stripes on my sleeves to signify my doctoral level. They watched me approach the podium as my name was called, as I was handed my diploma and then stood with my back to my Dissertation Chairman as he ceremonially placed the burnt orange and white doctoral hood over the awkward square, flat mortarboard balanced on top of my head, its gold tassel blowing in the breeze. As they watched, a part of me moved proudly through all of those time-honored rituals, while another part of me was so shocked it was a struggle to not float out of my body.

My two worlds collided in that one heart-stopping instant. I was filled with both the deepest sadness and the greatest sense of accomplishment I had ever experienced. My fate and my destiny appeared together in that one pivotal moment, giving me a choice about how I wanted my future to unfold. I would realize later that my graduation signified not only earning my PhD but also my initiation into my own reality, my truer identity, my consciously chosen destiny.

* * *

My first *Rupture* did not happen in one moment in time. I wouldn't have been able to handle that. Instead, the force of it shot through me in spurts, in layers with intervals of time in between. Each impact corresponded to my willingness for another layer of denial to be ripped away. This process was not forced on me—instead, the speed and strength of it stayed in concert with my acceptance of each new revelation, every step of the way. The evolution of consciousness is a dance between *The Great Artist* and the evolving self. It is co-created. How very gracious.

* * *

Things happened pretty quickly after that. The Monday after my graduation, I called my lawyer and filed for divorce. Four days later, the psychologist that I had interviewed with for my first internship called back and offered me a position in her private practice. The divorce was finalized on February 28 of the following year.

QUESTIONS FOR SELF-REFLECTION

1. This chapter is about the differences between our fate and our destiny. Can you describe the differences between the two? Every *Rupture* offers the choice between continuing to live out of our fates or abandoning them to step into our destinies. In reflecting on your own life, can you see which choices you made between these two potential future paths with each of your *Ruptures*? Where did those choices lead you?

2. After my first major *Rupture*, I was so undone that I had to ask my whole family to come and stay with me until I could find a new footing in my life. Have you ever had to ask for some serious help from the people close to you? What was that experience like for you?

3. In your mind, how is choosing to step through a *Rupture in the Canvas* a way to participate in our own evolution?

4. I approached the Greek Orthodox monastery in Blanco with openness and curiosity. Have you ever moved into a space of pure openness, where you let go of all of your normal assumptions about life and how it's supposed to work? What prompted that kind of abandon in your own life and where did it lead you?

5. What role does prayer have in your life, or not? Have you ever surprised yourself with prayer? Have you ever had a prayer answered?

A DEEPER LOOK #1

CHAPTER FIVE

THE TREASURE

*The kingdom is like a merchant looking for fine pearls.
When he had found one pearl of great price,
He went and sold all that he had and bought it.*

- Jesus, Matthew 13:45-46

I am putting the linear narrative of my life on pause again for a moment to circle back around to a particular decision in my life that catapulted me into a whole new level of consciousness. I want to put a frame around that decision, bringing you with me as I crawl inside its bracketed image to look very closely at all of its components. I now know that particular choice carried with it a lifetime of consequences. It took place at that fateful New Year's Eve party where I decided to play with matches, stretching past the boundary of my marriage vows.

I have already shared with you how this decision was related to the downfall of my marriage. But this time, I want to take you deep inside of me, to show you how that decision affected me personally in a way that had nothing to do with my relationship with Josh. On the one hand, this decision is humiliating to talk about. It still embarrasses me. On the other hand, acting so out of character woke me up in a most unexpected way. In *Great Artist* terms, that decision is a perfect example of my **Nancy-self** leaving the **Foyer**, walking right past the clacking and chanting of the three **Hungry Ghosts**, and entering the **Studio** to take my place in front of the **Collective Collage** to add some of my very own images.

It's not like I hadn't painted any of my own unique images on the **Canvas** before. I had. As I have already mentioned, the decision to leave *The Church* as well as the decision to go to graduate school were two very real examples. But this time was different. Although those precious independent decisions both marked a change in my life, those images were respectable. They nestled neatly in the spaces between the existing drawings. With this bold act of self-indulgence at the New Year's Eve party, I didn't care if my new image fit in neatly or not. I marched into the **Studio**, grabbed a brush out of the water, dipped it in bright red acrylic, and painted graffiti in bold strokes all over the original **Collage**. I was tired of being good and quiet and still. For once, I wanted to be wild and crazy, to do what I wanted to do without worrying about its effect on anybody else. I suddenly didn't care whether it was right or good or responsible. The truth is I wanted to feel what it felt like to be desired. And I loved it.

I now see that this act of self-will was an essential part of my personal evolution. I needed to rip off the straitjacket I had lived in my whole life. I needed to experience myself separate from its restrictive constraints. My **Maggie-self** had been my dominant identity up to that point in my life, but a secret part of me knew she wasn't my real truth. She wasn't me. Knowing that intellectually on some level didn't have the power to break me out of it, however. It had to be experienced—cellularly. So, when I had the opportunity to push right past the boundaries of propriety and decorum, right past the walls of the sanctuary, I seized upon it. Although I could not have possibly known it then, I know now that spontaneous act of self-gratification was a necessary step in finding my way to a deeper truth.

Here comes the surprising part. After the initial exhilaration, I moved into a state of intense confusion. I felt an inner turmoil with two parts of myself pulling me in opposite directions. A part of me was still caught up in the fun of it all, while another part of me began to feel heavy. I slowly sank into a dark corner. This wasn't because I felt guilty for breaking a rule (*Maggie* felt guilty, of course, but *Nancy* was happy to keep painting), but because I could feel in my cells and in my bones, in the full core of my body, a violation of something sacred that lived inside of me. That something is called *my truth*. For the first time in my life, I realized that I carried within me an inner truth meter—one that wasn't prescribed by the *Hungry Ghosts*. And it, all on its own, was signaling to me, my *Nancy-self*, that I had ventured off-course. It was a felt-sense experience—not at all conceptual. At first, I didn't know what to do with it.

Up until that viscerally felt violation, I had known what to do because of what I had been taught by some outside authority. I was very familiar with feeling guilty or shameful for breaking a prescribed rule, but this was different. Violating something sacred inside of me that was deserving of my respect and reverence made me feel sick inside, a sickness that eventually could not be ignored. And it was at that point I knew what I needed to do to bring myself into alignment. I knew what I *wanted* to do. This kind of knowing/wanting was entirely new to me. That moment of clarity brought all of my parts together—mind, body, heart and *Soul* coalesced into one. I was forever changed by that experience. For the very first time in my life, I moved into my *Soul-self*, but I couldn't have articulated it at the time.

I have to say: ironically, my decision to rip off my straitjacket resulted in one of the most important lessons I have learned along the way because for the first time, I came into contact with an internal guidance system that I didn't know was there. Alarm bells! Not the old familiar ones that cautioned me back into fear, guilt, and shame. No, these alarm bells sounded different. They felt different. Amazingly, these newly discovered alarm bells were connected to the truth, of all things. What an unexpected and gracious gift.

* * *

In the middle of all of that inner turmoil, I recognized that I had been born with an internal truth meter. It was my first experience with a reservoir of Holistic Wisdom and Unconditional Love. And this takes us full circle, back to the very beginning of the book, back to that indefinable liminal space I talked about in the Preface:

There is a quiet, open space inside myself where I often hear the Voice. Sometimes it speaks to me when I ask a direct question. Other times it comes in the form of a Vision or as a Character in a dream, personified as an Angel or a Guide, or a Soul Keeper. Sometimes I just feel its presence in my body. Regardless of its presentation, I don't experience it as my voice and it's not a voice that is audible out there in the world. That is, this other Voice, this other Viewpoint, does not come from the part of me I identify with most of the time, which lives on a roller coaster of felt sensations and heartfelt emotions. That's the me I identify with most of the time. This other Voice of the "Divine Ones," this other Energy, is always bigger and broader and deeper, steadier and more peaceful, more wholistic in its vantage point. And it is that bigger-than vantage point that I have come to rely upon.

I can't tell you for certain Who or What it is that is always eager to bring me messages from some Wholistic viewpoint. Who or What it is doesn't matter to me. That this Source is there and available and wants to send me messages is all that counts. It made itself known to me for the first time when I violated my own personal truth. It signaled to me, loud and clear, through a sick feeling that encompassed the whole of my body. I didn't *hear* it as a Voice that time. I *felt* it energetically, viscerally, just like an inner compass with an alarm bell on it signaling I had veered off-course. It showed up all on its own, organically built into the system. And, although it didn't feel like another being, it was undoubtedly loving—unconditionally loving—and clearly only wanted my highest good.

Since that first conscious encounter with this Loving Presence, it has presented itself to me in a number of forms. Often, as I have said, personified as an Angel or a Spirit Guide or in the form of that dependable, wise inner Voice. Surely, *The Great Artist* is one of its guises. How it shows up is irrelevant. That it does, that it is there with me, is what I have come to rely upon. I consider it my greatest treasure. And even though I can go unconscious and forget about it for a while, truth be told, it's the only thing that really matters to me.

QUESTIONS FOR SELF-REFLECTION

1. What actions in your past bring you the greatest sense of shame? How do you relate to the part of you who behaved in those ways now?

2. When I "acted out" at that New Year's Eve party, part of me was rebelling against a strict religious upbringing. I was rebelling against an outer authority. The first stage toward healing started to sink in when I realized that my act of rebellion didn't free me from anything. It tied me in knots. Can you relate to a time when you began to realize that you, and not something or someone outside of yourself, were the cause of your own suffering?

3. The title of this chapter is "The Treasure." During this time in my life, I discovered that my greatest treasure of all was my connection to a Loving Presence. Do you know what your greatest treasure is? How did you come to recognize it?

4. Do you know what I mean about the differences between acting out of guilt and acting from a place of inner truth? How do you relate to those differences?

5. In this chapter, I have explained that an act of self-indulgence was a necessary step in my personal evolution. Ironically, that self-serving act turned out to be the opening to a whole new level of awareness for me. Through it, I discovered that I had an inner truth meter. Have you experienced making a choice that you thought would take you in one direction,

but which took you someplace entirely differently, that took you to an experience with a hidden gift in it? What does this tell you, if anything, about the nature of life?

THE SECOND RUPTURE

CHAPTER SIX

FLYING SOLO

We can be free!
We can learn to fly!

- Richard Bach -

The decision to follow **The Great Artist** through his gaping tear leads to unknown territory. The first time I made that decision, I was quite surprised by what I began to experience in my life on the **Back Side of the Canvas**. What I know now, after five more **Ruptures**, is that we can't generalize what we might encounter on the **Back Side**. That's the whole point of it. Each pass-through takes each of us somewhere entirely new and unpredictable, which relates to the number of images that have been slashed and the depth of meaning they carry. The degree of disorientation on the **Back Side of the Rupture** is in concert with how much of our worldview or identity has been affected by **The Great Artist's** defilement. Another way to put it is that the degree of disorientation on the **Back Side of the Canvas** is dependent upon the tenacity of our attachment to the images that have been decimated.

As I have already mentioned, this first **Rupture** was the most painful and therefore left me with the greatest disorientation. I had to gradually adjust to my new surroundings. This was really uncomfortable. Eventually, I did find new footing and began to receive the gifts from that phase of my journey.

*   *   *

Before graduation, I had contacted Dr. Joanna Carver to see if she would be willing to supervise my post-doctorate internship. Although she had originally told me that her internship spaces were full, she called me back a few days after I filed for divorce to tell me that a space had opened up after all. It was mine if I wanted it and it would start the following Monday. My body reverberated with both terror and excitement as I accepted the position.

On that first Monday, I ran back and forth to the bathroom all morning, couldn't eat my breakfast for fear I might throw up. I frantically prayed all the way to the downtown high-rise, not knowing how I could possibly be a therapist to someone else. The *Hungry Ghosts* screamed at me, "Do you honestly think you are ready to be a therapist? Who are you kidding? You have no idea what you are doing. What if you have to go to the bathroom in the middle of your session?! You're a complete wreck, a fraud, a weakling!" The incessant *clack, clack, clacking* continued as the *Bookkeeper* tallied up all my shortcomings.

I kept breathing and praying. "Holy Spirit, you have got to help me! I can't do this by myself! I'm terrified! I'm sick! Help me!" This prayer came straight from my *Maggie-self*. When she prays, she's always frantic. My *Nancy-self*'s prayer is calmer but just as fervent: "I know nothing. Show me." I alternated between my frantic prayer and my calmer prayer while I got dressed.

Inside myself, that internal Voice that I was beginning to rely upon simply said, "Nancy, all you have to do is get your body there. We'll do the rest. Remember Moses?" In my mind's eye, I saw a vision of Moses standing at the burning bush, pleading to the Great I Am, who had just asked him to free

His people from the bondage of the mighty Egyptians. I realize the hubris in even beginning to compare my situation with Moses's, but that's the image that came up.

"Please don't ask me to do this," pleaded Moses. "I'm not capable. I have a speech impediment," he implored. "Send someone else. Send my brother, Aaron. He's more eloquent than I am." And in response to his pleading, Moses was told, "Just go see the pharaoh. We'll do the rest."

I drove myself to the Omni Hotel and office complex on the corner of San Jacinto and 7th Street in downtown Austin. Up until this point in my life, I didn't have much reason to go downtown. It was always congested. The parking was impossible. I wasn't used to the pace and vibe of the hip, professional Type A's who worked down there. I lived on the outskirts of the city, on the crest of the Texas Hill Country. My familiar stomping grounds had been our suburban neighborhood and the UT campus. I was entering foreign territory on more than one front.

I drove into the adjacent covered garage with my valued parking permit hanging from the rearview mirror, found my way to the Omni's entrance, and followed the signs to the spacious lobby. The smell of freshly roasted coffee from the French café permeated the entire area, wafting up the long escalator along with me as I made my way to the second floor that housed the professional offices. I found office suite 202 and entered the waiting room. I told Susan, the receptionist at the sliding glass window, who I was and why I was there. She asked me to wait for a moment. Another woman sat in the waiting room with me. We glanced at each other and smiled. She was pleasant. I wondered if she could tell how scared I was. I wondered where the bathroom was.

Susan escorted me back to Dr. Carver's office. Dr. Carver stood up from her desk to greet me, dressed to the nines in a lime-green linen suit and glistening black patent pumps. She welcomed me to the practice and then gave me a short tour of the suite. She showed me where the copier was, the breakroom, and where the files were kept. She then escorted me to my new psychotherapy office, informing me that my first client was waiting for me and that Susan would send her in at 9:00.

Already?! My new mentor was throwing me into the deep end from the very start. Outwardly, I held myself together, but inwardly, I was quaking. Although I had done a nine-month practicum in the student counseling center at Austin Community College, I still did not at all feel prepared to meet with the general public. I felt my *Maggie-self* go weak at the knees and begin to crater inside. "Help me! Help me! Help me!" she frantically pleaded. I felt my *Nancy-self* hold her own as she silently repeated, "I know nothing. Show me."

At 9:00, Susan escorted my first client into the room. She introduced us and then returned to the reception desk, leaving me alone in the room with this stranger. I recognized her as the woman in the waiting room. I asked her to sit across from me and to tell me a little bit about why she was seeking therapy and how I could help. She started with, "Oh, I saw you in the waiting room. You looked so calm. You helped me to calm down."

Ha! Little did she know how badly I wanted to switch chairs with her and pour out all of my angst for her listening ears. I took a deep breath and thanked my Guides for reassuring me through her words. She then went on to share with me about her relationship with her husband, how she didn't know how to hold onto herself when he became angry, how she felt weak inside. I settled into my chair and felt my body relax as I reflected back her feelings, honestly able to empathize with her situation. Maybe I was prepared after all.

My first day as a therapist was one of many firsts that I experienced after stepping through that first *Rupture in the Canvas*. The years after my divorce took me to places inside myself I didn't know existed, as well as unfamiliar places out there in the world. After a whole lot of initial terror and self-doubt, I slowly discovered more of *me* detaching from my enmeshed identity with Josh. Amazingly, over time, I began to enjoy my own company. I really liked what I liked. I felt an increasing inner strength. I gained confidence in my practice as a therapist, as a single mom, and as an individual in my own right. These are all examples of my experiencing a stronger belief in myself, part of that ego-building process that I mentioned in the last chapter. I was continuing to align myself with the destiny of my truth as opposed to the fate of my childhood assumptions, and I was finding that alignment based on my internal experience.

This strength-building would serve me for the rest of my life. But I have to admit, the beginning of the process was rough and rocky, unsteady, filled with spurts of flight followed by crash landings, sort of like one of those clumsy puffins you see on the Nature Channel, graceful in the air but landing in big belly-flops on the beach.

Being a single parent brought with it a whole new benchmark. Emmie, our oldest, had graduated from high school the summer before our divorce was final. She was thrilled to be leaving home, to get away from all the tension and drama our family had experienced over the preceding two years. She was heading to the University of Colorado in Boulder, our favorite vacation spot. Colorado was more than familiar; it was like our home away from home. The mountains, the pines, the rushing rivers had always brought us a sense of connection.

In late August of 1994, Josh and I drove Emmie to her new school. Together. Though we were formally separated and in the middle of our divorce settlement, we were both committed to being with Emmie as she left home for the first time. I stocked up on whodunnit mysteries and stand-up comedy tapes to play in the car on the way up there. (Yes, I said tapes. Podcasts were still years away!) They helped to replace the tension in the air with chatter, as none of us felt much like talking during the two-day trip.

Josh and I both helped Emmie unpack, then we did the customary Target run and room set-up. We toured the campus, ate lunch at a fun restaurant on Pearl Street, and gave her big bear hugs and kisses on the cheek with our tearful goodbyes. And then I took a taxi to the airport as Josh drove back to his home at the lake house. We did a pretty good job of working together as co-parents, both of us dearly loving our daughter, our hearts aching but full.

That left Cade and Jack at home with me during the week and with Josh on most weekends out at the lake house. I became a working mom for the very first time in their lives. This brought a whole new set of firsts. The weekend before my first Monday on the job, I went into overdrive at home, making a huge batch of breakfast tacos: flour tortillas filled with scrambled eggs, ground sausage, and lots of cheddar cheese for the boys to microwave anytime they were hungry. I was obsessed with keeping all the balls in the air. It was all on me now and I didn't want to screw it up. I felt so responsible.

But over time, this whole thing became exhausting, not to mention impossible. Over time, I calmed down, dropped my Superwoman cape, and bought frozen pizza pockets, which I am embarrassed to admit became a staple in their diet. I realized I couldn't do it all by myself. I had to cut some corners to keep us all afloat. I decided to let myself be human. Just be human. Somehow, we all managed through the learning curve and eventually settled into a new routine.

Three years after Emmie left, I drove Cade the hour and a half down the road to Texas A&M University. He was excited about getting in, loved all the Aggie traditions, and had some friends going there with him. After the Target run and setting up his room, we went to Freebirds for one of their Texas-size two-handed burritos. When I was dropping him off in the parking lot back on campus, he paused. His hand was on the door handle but he couldn't move. He was frozen in that transitional space between holding on to the last vestiges of home and launching forth into this new adventure. He said, "I know I'll be fine once I get out of the car, but I just can't make myself open the door." I sat quietly with him as he struggled inside himself. I placed my hand on his and gently said, "It's time, Cade. It's time. You're going to love it." At that, he pulled the door handle and stepped out of the car. I got out to give him a big hug, tears streaming down both of our faces. And off he went.

Jack was home for four more years after Cade left. We had a great time, just the two of us. He had lots of friends, did great in school, and let his hair grow long and curly. His dad let him bring friends with him out to the lake on the weekends. He learned to drive and started borrowing my car. Forever the night owl, Jack's favorite thing to do was knock on my door at around 10:40 at night and say, "Hey Momma, we have just enough time to make it to Amy's (the local ice cream shop) before they close." Invariably, I would throw on an old pair of jeans and jump in the car for the twelve-minute drive to Amy's. I have bittersweet memories of those late-night trips with Jack, the baby of the family. I knew all too well that he too would be leaving before we knew it.

Over the years, each of the three kids did take his or her turn at throwing themselves into situations that stretched me beyond any place I had ever gone before and, naively, ever thought I would have to. By then, we were no longer pretending to be that picture-perfect family. Everything that happened—the good, the bad, and the ugly—was just laid out there in full view. We dealt with it all the best we could. For the first time, I realized that the tension in our family didn't stem from just the strife between Josh and me, but from all the effort it took to keep the charade going. That's what we dropped. We finally all let go of the pretty picture. It was such an unexpected relief.

Emmie went into a dark hole after breaking up with her college boyfriend. With his self-respect momentarily replaced by freshman freedom, Cade got a ticket for peeing off the balcony of the motel while on Spring Break with 5,000 other college coeds at Padre Island. And some years later, Jack had to spend a few hours in the San Angelo, Texas jailhouse for driving through town in his open-air Jeep, his CU sticker on the bumper, his curly, woolly locks flapping in the breeze while in possession of less than two ounces of marijuana. (I never thought I would need to know how to contact a bail bondsman before, but now I can say I am experienced.)

Each one of these experiences threw me for a loop, jangled at my mama heartstrings while at the same time stretching me a little further toward falling in love with truth. Our family was certainly less picture-perfect than we appeared in the portrait that still hung on the wall of our neighborhood diner, but at least we weren't living on perfumed, stale air anymore. Despite my motherly concern and my ever-present self-doubt, we just began to take things as they were, one day at a time.

* * *

While Jack was still in high school, I discovered a little twenty-four-hour chapel that I passed every day going to and from work. I would sometimes stop and go inside when I felt the need to step out of my life and just sit and breathe. This quiet respite provided a transition between work and home.

Overarching pine trees surround the chapel. Needle-leafed branches nod through the rectangular pane-glass window on the back wall just above the large, rustic wooden cross. A row of alfresco windows lining each side of the tiny structure remains open except in the winter, allowing in the scent of nearby roses and pines. One of my visits from those transition years stands out clearly in my memory.

I took a seat on one of the pews about three rows back from the altar and began to allow prayers to filter through my mind and heart as the gentle breeze wafted through the open air. Keeping my focus on the cross, I sank into a meditative state that felt calm and reassuring. Then, all of a sudden, I saw something move. It was fast and caught me off guard. I didn't know what it was at first. I sat still, keeping my eyes open, waiting to see if it would happen again. After a few moments, in soared a brown-feathered mama wren—carrying dinner for her baby hatchlings. In she flew, straight to her nest, which perched on the horizontal beam of the hand-hewn cross. As soon as she reached the nest, three tiny necks stretched as high as they could, balancing downy, bobbling, round heads, gaping beaks open wide, begging to be filled. She shared her bounty with her chicks and then flew off to find them more.

And so there it was—a picture of perfect safety brought to me with its reassuring message: *All is well, Mama. See, all is well. You have built your nest on Holy Ground. It will support you. It will support your babies. Fly, Mama...fly out into the world on your very own wings and then fly back again. We'll hold them safe while you fly. We'll hold them safe. All is well. All is well.*

Tears came as I felt my heart opening.

After watching this Angel-bird and her babies for a few more minutes, I walked back to my car. As I drove home, I called Jack on my cell phone and told him to wait at the house. I smile at this memory now. Those were the days when my cell phone was as large as a hammer and just as heavy. And to think I used to carry that thing around with me in my purse! I called Jack to tell him I had a surprise for him.

When I got home, I honked from the driveway. Jack jumped in the car, but I wouldn't tell him where we were headed. As we approached the chapel, Jack recognized the route and assumed we were just going in to sit in the silence as we had done together a few times in the past. I stayed quiet and just asked him to go inside with me. We sat in the same pew where I had been before. We sat in the quiet. And then there she was again. The mama bird darted through the window and flew straight to her anchored nest. Her little ones raised their heavy, oversized heads and stretched their beaks to beg. Jack saw her and instinctively jumped to his feet, then quietly tiptoed in his size-twelve sneakers up to the altar. When mama bird flew out for another trip, Jack slipped off his shoes and climbed gingerly onto the sturdy wooden altar to peek inside the nest. Knowing that the bulk of the altar would not falter with his weight, I just sat back and watched, smiling and soaking it all in.

After we had had our fill of wonder, Jack and I headed to the car and then to Holiday House, his favorite hamburger place just down the street. He ordered his usual Fiesta Burger with chili and cheese—no onions, please. Life resumed its natural state as we sat in our favorite booth and shared the happenings of our day, but we both knew we had just gone to Heaven.

For the first time in the years since my divorce, on that magical day in the chapel, I knew that I wasn't really alone and we were all going to be okay. Just like the mama bird, our nest was cradled in something much stronger and far more transcendent than I was. I could finally exhale.

QUESTIONS FOR SELF-REFLECTION

1. Have you ever had to start completely over in your life, to claim a whole new identity? Was it exciting? Terrifying? Both? How did you face that?

2. When we dare to follow *The Great Artist* through a *Rupture in the Canvas*, we never know what life will be like on the other side. What we do know is that it will be qualitatively different from anything we have known before. Think about the major *Ruptures* in your own life. Can you identify some of the qualitative differences between your life before and after your first *Rupture*? How did your life change as a result of it, energetically, practically, and spiritually? Consider who or what the authority figures in your life were before and after, or look at what you valued before a *Rupture* and how that value system changed after it.

3. Life on the *Back Side of the Canvas* is all about living more out of one's experience of the truth rather than out of an image of how the self or one's life should look. If you have lived through at least one major *Rupture*, in which specific ways did it change your relationship to truth?

4. Once I started praying my *Nancy*-prayer, I began to look for outward signs and clues from my Guides. I interpreted the mama bird as a message from the Source of Loving Wisdom that my new life with my kids was built on solid ground, we were all okay, and I was not alone. Do you resonate with this sort of relationship with whatever you call sacred, or does this feel foreign to you?

CHAPTER SEVEN

WHITE STONES IN THE MOONLIGHT

*The moment one definitely commits oneself,
then providence moves too. All sorts of things occur
to help one that would never otherwise
have occurred...
Unforeseen incidents, meetings, and material assistance,
which no man could have dreamed
would have come his way.*

- W. H. Murray -

A key component to my journey into independence was my evolving relationship and dependence on the Divine, whatever that means. My connection was continually called into place through my two fervent prayers, one from **Maggie**—"Help me! Help me! Help me!"—and the other from my **Nancy-self**: "I know nothing. Show me." Both expressed my powerlessness and my willingness for Spirit to intervene.

Although I have mentioned this decision before, I haven't shared the details of it. As far as my more formal faith was concerned, Josh and I left *The Church* of our childhood when we were in our late twenties. Although one might expect our leaving *The Church* to count as a major **Rupture** in my life, it wasn't. Both of my sisters had already left, and Josh's and my parting came more as a gradual emergence than an abrupt break. We just grew out of it. This move wasn't long after I first heard the alarm bells of truth as I processed the events of the New Year's Eve party. As I got deeper in touch with my inner guidance, there came a time when I just knew I couldn't stay in *The Church* anymore—could no longer support its rigidity, its literalism, or its exclusivity. Yet it was all I knew of organized religion. So, I began to question everything. Was all that stuff about Jesus really true? Virgin birth? Water into wine? Walking on water? Raised from the dead? Really? I kept hunting for the right box to put Jesus in. And because I couldn't find it, I just put him in a holding tank someplace deep inside of me. I didn't go and visit there very often. I essentially moved into agnosticism.

In those early years after leaving *The Church*, I never let go of my belief, my experience of Something Greater than I was, even though I could no longer envision it in a structured way. I felt untethered and began to explore Carl Jung's depth psychology, Buddhism through the lens of Thích Nhất Hạnh, Tara Brach, John Woodward, and the Dalai Lama, and was eventually led back to my Christian roots through *A Course in Miracles*.

The *Course* was my way back to a form of Christianity that made sense to me. It keeps in all the love but filters out the fear, guilt, and shame that was so prevalent in my experience of the gospel message of fundamentalist Christianity. By the time of my separation and divorce and well beyond, the *Course* had become the bedrock of my life as well as the foundation of my work with clients. A key component of the *Course* is the Workbook that accompanies the primary text. The Workbook presents a thought for every day of the year meant to be used as a centering mantra for meditation. This focused practice launched me into a daily meditation practice that continues to this day. That and journaling is what keeps me connected to that Divine Presence. It's what keeps me sane. Many years later, I would move the *Course* to the side wings and embrace a more feminine aspect of that invisible Force, focusing more on the body, heart, and *Soul* rather than simply a spiritual oneness with the All. But that journey is for another time.

It was during the years that I was making my way on my own that I had *The Great Artist Dream*. A few years later I had what I call the *Jesus Download Dream*. Just like *The Great Artist Dream*, the *Jesus Download Dream* came as an unexpected gift.

The Jesus Download Dream

I am at a huge conference for people seeking psycho-spiritual transformation. It is held at a giant, fancy hotel somewhere. There are hundreds if not thousands of people in attendance. Jesus is to be the keynote speaker. It is commonly known that he has been sentenced to prison and, as such, has been living in some sort of dungeon somewhere. He is only being temporarily released, just long enough to give his talk and then to be escorted back to the dungeons.

In the opening scene, I am in a large reception area waiting to see him. I have gotten word that he is looking for both me and my friend and mentor, Frank Allen. Jesus is excited to have a chance to see us and we can't wait to see him. I catch a glimpse of Frank at a distance, across the great expanse of the ballroom. He sees me and waves. I am delighted to see that he is leading Jesus in my direction. I am so excited. I feel so honored that Jesus is looking for me. He and Frank and I are old friends.

When they get to me, Jesus and I look into each other's eyes, smile in recognition, and then give each other a great big hug. I realize as we hold the embrace that Jesus is beginning to transmit "information" to me straight into my heart, my body, into my Soul—that intuitive-gut space. I start to question him about it, but before I can speak, I hear telepathically, "Nancy, just stand still. Hold on tight. I don't have time to send this to your brain first. It would take too long for you to understand it with your mind. We don't have time for all of that. You're getting it. It's just that your head will be the last to know. Just trust me." So, I sort of smile and hold still within his embrace while Jesus bypasses my conscious mind and downloads divine wisdom directly into my accepting heart.

* * *

It's so telling that the *Jesus Download Dream* starts with Jesus being released from his dungeon prison so that he can give the keynote address to a large gathering. I can't help but laugh at how blunt the dream is about where "my" Jesus lived most of the time. No pussy-footing around, no punches held back to protect my feelings or image of myself. No, the dream is clear about where I kept Jesus at that time in my life.

It is also true that both in the dream and when I woke up, I had no idea what kind of sacred data had been "downloaded." None of it reached the level of consciousness.

But what was most telling about the dream was how I felt in it and when I woke up from it.

In the dream, I was genuinely eager to see Jesus and he was as eager to see me. We hadn't seen each other for a long time. It's as if one of us had moved away. That would be me. I was the one who had moved away from him when I left my fundamentalist roots. The whole Jesus-thing had turned into a great, big, stupid, sickening wadded-up mess. And although I had been a student of the *Course*, which is supposedly written from the voice of Jesus, I still did not have a clear picture of who or what he really was out there in the world, much less inside myself. So, I kept him secretly tucked away in an inner dungeon.

But maybe that was the whole point. Maybe the dream was brought to show me that my head doesn't have to know how to categorize him. Maybe I didn't have to *figure him out* to come to peace with him.

In the dream, when I heard that Jesus was being released to speak at the conference, I was spontaneously delighted to see him. I couldn't wait. I didn't stop to think about it. I was just really glad. And when I saw that Frank was leading him in my direction, that they were also looking for me—for me in particular—I felt my heart sing a little tune as it opened to greet him.

Then we hugged a great big friend-to-friend hug. And right

in the middle of that embrace, Jesus sent me messages or information or activated a hidden reservoir. What he did inside that hug, I didn't know, but what I did know was that I wanted it. I wanted what he wanted to give me. And I felt that *wanting* in my cells and in my bones, in my heart and in my **Soul**. And it warmed me from the inside out. In the dream, I *felt* who he was to me. And I was glad that my head didn't have a vote.

* * *

As was true with *The Great Artist Dream*, the meaning of the *Jesus Download Dream* has deepened and expanded over the years. Looking back on it now, so many years later, I hold the dream as a validation of my conscious choice to trust in a Divine Source rather than in my ability to figure things out. The dream showed me that even when my rational mind doesn't understand something, I will be shown through other channels. The necessary information will be brought my way. It will come as an unexpected gift if I am willing to receive it.

In *The Great Artist Dream*, after the initial devastating shock of the **Rupture**, I chose to follow **The Great Artist** through the **Canvas**. In the *Jesus Download Dream*, I chose to hold still while Jesus infiltrated my being with something sacred. In this second dream, I am not in a state of shock like in the first. I am in a state of eager anticipation and an open willingness to accept whatever he has to give me. My receptive **Nancy-self** is in charge.

At the point in my life when I had this dream, I had already moved into a more open willingness to whatever life had to give me. I accepted the lead of the Sacred, in all of its myriad forms, or at least that was my earnest intention. Of course, I went back and forth on this, but through the *Jesus Download Dream*, I was being shown something different about that relationship. Looking back on it now, I see it as the solidification of a lifelong treasure hunt that my rational mind couldn't begin to understand, much less direct. I was beginning to realize this was what it felt like to live more consciously and consistently in the *Space Behind the Canvas*. I was beginning to surrender more readily into the depths of humility and trust. I was learning through experience that we can't enter the *Space Behind the Canvas* when we think we know what we will find there. Properly stepping through the *Canvas* requires the *Nancy-self*'s familiar position of "I know nothing. Show me."

Asking to be shown requires some degree of faith. The Bible says that all that is required to move a mountain is faith the size of a mustard seed. I have found this to be true. The bulk of me can be all caught up in my *Maggie-self*'s fears and self-doubt, or in my *Nancy-self*'s readiness to paint her own picture of reality when she first enters the *Studio*, while another part, my authentic *Soul-self*, tiny as she might be in comparison, can hold the faith for all of me. And that is all that is required.

Life on the *Back Side of the Canvas* is not rehearsed. It is not patterned through concepts, ideals, or values that we have been taught. It is open and free, yet safe and benevolent. I have found that living life on the *Back Side of the Canvas* is like dancing with a skilled partner, like *The Great Artist* or Jesus or Sophia, Buddha, the Great Mother, or the Holy Spirit—regardless of the name of the thing, it's always the Creative Life-Force taking the lead and me following every nuanced gesture or grand, sweeping dip. It's like following white stones in the moonlight, like Hansel and Gretel, who find their way back home one stone at a time. Life doesn't give us a five-year plan. It simply gives us one glistening stone at a time. It is our job to pick it up, let it penetrate our lives, and then be on the lookout for discovering the next.

The *Jesus Download Dream* was telling me to stop living so much out of my head. Stop trying to figure it all out. Stop working so hard at painting images on the *Canvas*. It told me to just stand still and let it be brought to me—that I would get what I needed, even if my head didn't understand it. That was its gift.

* * *

Once I started living out of this partnership more consistently, unexpected encounters started showing up in my life.

During my separation, although my primary spiritual path had become *A Course in Miracles*, I started going to a Sunday school class at a non-denominational church not far from where I lived. Some Sundays, I would go to the formal service in the sanctuary, but most of the time, I just went to the adult Sunday school class taught by Dr. Bob Lively. Bob was an assistant minister at the church, held his Divinity degree from Austin Presbyterian Theological Seminary, and was certified as a pastoral counselor. I loved Bob's class. He taught a Christianity that was open and smart, filled with love and grace—quite the contrast from *The Church* of my childhood. Bob's messages were progressive, ecumenical, and always spiced with a relevant down-home story from his growing-up years. Bob is a great storyteller.

One Sunday morning, a cute, petite blonde approached me with a smile and introduced herself as Suzanne. She had noticed that I had been coming to Bob's class on my own, as had she. We went to lunch together that day, which marked the beginning of a long-term friendship. During that first conversation, I realized Suzanne was not just cute and petite and blonde. She was brilliant, holding a degree in Chemical Engineering! I also learned that she too had experienced her own **Rupture** through a devastating divorce. And, just like me, that experience had led her to fall in love with truth. We felt an instant connection. Suzanne became my first new friend on the **Back Side of the Canvas**. Although, she now lives in another state, that brilliant, cute, petite Suzanne is one of my dearest friends to this day. She came into my life as a surprise package—as a lasting gift.

One Sunday morning, Bob announced that he was going to be leading a singles' retreat. I didn't think much about it, as I wasn't even formally divorced yet and certainly didn't identify myself as "single," but Suzanne had been divorced for about a year so she asked me if I would go with her. I told her that I would, not because I was interested in meeting men, but because I wanted to spend time with her and to learn more from Bob.

During a break on that retreat, I ended up bumping into Bob along a path that surrounded the retreat grounds. As we walked, we got better acquainted. This allowed me to tell Bob how much I appreciated his view of theology and how refreshing it was to hear, given my background. He told me about his starting a soup kitchen in a disadvantaged area of South Dallas. I shared that I was a new psychotherapist, working for the first time in a private practice setting. I talked with him about my dissertation, how I had interviewed people who had gone through a life-changing event, how I was interested in the event's effect on their relationship to a personal God-image. We both listened as we discovered the similarities in our spiritual take on life and our experience in working with clients. At the end of our walk, Bob asked me if I had a business card. He wanted to start referring clients to me. And he did. Bob became my primary referral source for the first five years of my practice. He single-handedly launched my career.

I didn't plan these encounters with Suzanne and Bob. They were brought my way.

Over the next five or so years, I settled into a new normal. One by one, all three kids went away to school and I went to work every day. I spent one year under Dr. Carver's supervision and then transitioned under the supervision of Dr. Frank Allen, the psychotherapist who had led the Spirit Quest retreat where I found clarity about confronting my marriage. Frank was a dedicated student and teacher of *A Course in Miracles*. I was a part of his *Course* group for many years and then became a part of a case consultation group that he led for practicing therapists. This group met once a month for twenty years.

It was also during this time that Frank began training under Dr. Brian Weiss, a psychiatrist who holds degrees from Columbia

University and Harvard Medical School. Through a fascinating discovery, while working with a patient, Weiss was launched into the world of reincarnation. After this life-altering experience, Weiss became an expert in past-life regression therapy. As a trainee, Frank learned Weiss's hypnotic induction technique and needed volunteers to practice on. He asked if I was game. I agreed without hesitation. This sounded like fun to me.

Neither of us knew if reincarnation was real or not, or even if we fully believed in that sort of take on things, but the *literal* reality of it was not as important to me as the *experience* of it. From our standpoint, it seemed that even if it were only *as if* in another lifetime such and such happened, it would hold as much meaning as it would if the whole thing had happened some decades or centuries before. My openness played a role, just as it did when I visited the weeping Mother Mary icon. I have learned that this unbiased space is a vital component of the evolutionary process. It is putting into action the **Nancy**-prayer, "I know nothing. Show me."

The first time Frank put me under, he led me into a deep, relaxed state, and then suggested that I go to some previous lifetime. While I expected to experience some past time on the planet Earth, I ended up in *Heaven*. I'm not quite sure how I knew it was Heaven. It was just an open, white space.

> *I left my body and started to float up, up, up. I found myself in Heaven. At first, Heaven didn't look like much. It was just an open space filled with a soft, shimmering light. I was just standing there, waiting, when a girl from my childhood came in from an angle. Kate was two years younger than I was and lived two doors down. We played together often, but one day she and her older sister refused to speak to me. They treated me as if I didn't exist and this was done without any explanation. We hadn't had a fight. Things had been amicable. It left me confused and deeply hurt. I felt so devalued, betrayed, unwanted. But in this vision of Heaven, Kate stood in front of me, folded her hands in*

Namaste fashion, bowed her head toward me, smiled, and said, "I played my part for you." I felt blessed by her presence.

And then one by one, everyone I had ever encountered in my whole life came in, bowed in front of me, smiled, and said, "I played my part for you." This went on until I knew that nothing in my life was left out. I knew that even a piece of dust in the corner of a room had played its part for me. All my pets, my friends, my not-so-friends, people who had adored me, and people who had ignored me—everybody, everything, nothing left out—all had played their parts for me. It was awesome! It was astounding! It was humbling and exhilarating! I loved it!

Then, just as I was grasping the impact of this experience, I found myself standing in front of each one of those who had come and bowed toward me to offer their blessing. There was my mother, my sisters, my father, my former husband, my children—my childhood friends and those who were to follow, those in my life I had loved, those I had judged or slighted, ignored or wronged, people I had only stood next to in an elevator. To each of them, I folded my hands in Namaste fashion, smiled, bowed my head, and said, "I played my part for you."

I couldn't fully make sense of this because the experience lay just beyond the edge of my rational mind. I did not rationally *understand* how the good, the bad, and the ugly could somehow be a blessing, but just like in the *Jesus Download Dream*, I could *feel* it. Somehow, I realized that underneath all of our outer, everyday preoccupations lay a gift in disguise. I could feel the perfection of it all—life's perfect oneness. I could see that no matter where you intersected, no matter the starting point, all roads led back to the whole—each of us harmoniously, benevolently playing a part for every other in some sort of sacred dance.

And that was it.

With Frank's hypnotic induction, I did not experience myself in Great Britain back in the 1800s or on a slave ship sailing toward the Americas. I did not find myself in a mansion or a hovel or a deer-hide tent. Instead, I found myself in a blank space of timelessness, a nothingness overflowing with inseparable connection. Surprisingly, graciously, I recognized this place as Heaven.

QUESTIONS FOR SELF-REFLECTION

1. I make a distinction in this chapter between three sources of information about the Divine: 1) formal religion, 2) what my mind tells me is true, and 3) an *experience* of something as Sacred. Do you identify with those three ways of understanding/relating to Something bigger than we are? Be specific.

2. Have you ever experienced a powerful guided meditation or a vision of some sort? If so, did it/they have any lasting effect(s) on you? Or do you feel uncomfortable with this type of experience?

3. What was your reaction to my vision of Heaven? Can you connect with the idea of each of us playing our part for the rest? Why or why not?

4. What was your experience of reading about my description of following white stones in the moonlight to lead me through the wilderness on the **Back Side of the Canvas**? Do you identify with this idea? If so, what white stones have you discovered on the **Back Side of the Canvas**? If not, how would you describe *your* experience of life on the **Back Side of the Canvas**? Yours may be very different from mine.

CHAPTER EIGHT

LIFE LESSON

*At critical junctures, outer trouble
and the inner need to grow
conspire to set each of us on a path
of awakening and intuition.*

- Michael Meade -

It was one of the hottest days in August in the summer of 1983. Josh and I had decided to take the kids camping out at Inks Lake, one of the seven man-made lakes that run like a string of pearls along the Colorado River in the Texas Hill Country. We set up our tent and then launched the boat on an early Friday afternoon.

The kids were young. Jack was just a toddler. We spent the hot afternoon pulling the big kids behind the boat on a giant, covered inner tube. They took turns going around and around until everyone was exhausted and the sun started to fall toward the horizon. About that time, a big wind picked up as thunderclouds approached from the north. Josh pulled the giant, water-logged inner tube back into the boat, set it up on the front seat section, and then revved up the speed to get us out of the water before the clouds burst. It didn't take a minute before the inner tube lifted off the front seat, launched into the air, and then came barreling down from the sky and bounced off the top of my head. I was stunned. I felt my neck compress and an immediate dull pain. I knew I was okay; my neck was not broken, but I felt dazed not only from the blow but from the shock of it happening so unexpectedly. Josh brought the boat to a stop, and after checking to see if I was okay, he tied the inner tube in place and motored us more slowly back to the boat ramp.

While that shocking accident was not a **Rupture**, it became the trailhead to an evolutionary path toward a new level of awakening. This awakening started with chronic neck pain, which continued through my marriage and for many years after the divorce.

* * *

After the original neck injury on the boat in 1983, the pain would periodically and unpredictably resurrect. When this happened, I would see my chiropractor or acupuncturist and it would calm down, only to flare up again some weeks, months, or sometimes years later. It came back in full vengeance in 2004, twenty-one years after the original injury. So, like other times in the past, I started my routine again: going to the chiropractor and the acupuncturist, taking Advil and Tylenol around the clock. I even consulted with a neurosurgeon who told me he couldn't help because it was inoperable. This particular pain cycle persisted off and on for the next two years.

In January of 2006, after exhausting all of my known resources, it finally occurred to me to ask the *pain* why it was back in my life and what I needed to learn from it. I remembered that Carl Jung once said that if a monster is chasing you in a dream, stop, turn around, and ask it who it is and what it wants. I decided to use this shift in relationship with my neck pain to possibly shed some light. It wouldn't hurt to ask.

To do this, I went back to Frank and asked him to "put me under" again. Rather than continuing to resist it, I decided to get curious about the pain. I decided to get to know it. Maybe moving into a dreamlike state might uncover some unconscious meaning to the pain. Or maybe this pain had something to do with a past life, either literally or metaphorically. Again, this was just an experiment, kind of like when I lifted all judgment while a Greek Orthodox nun asked Mother Mary to bring me clarity about my marriage. There is something to that space of complete openness. I wasn't a true believer in reincarnation, and I also didn't know what happened in a typical past-life regression session since my only experience with it involved going to Heaven, but I was open to exploration.

It is important to note that stepping into that space of openness is much harder to do when we are still very attached to certain, cherished images on the *Canvas*. In other words, despite what we might like to think of ourselves and our level of awareness, we will inevitably still believe in some of the images as if they are real. This will become more clear in the chapters to follow. But in this situation with my neck pain, I was genuinely open.

After Frank led me into a deep, relaxed state of consciousness, he suggested that I leave my body and travel to another time that might be related to my current neck pain.

I immediately found myself in the middle of an arena where a martial arts competition was being held. This was someplace over in the Far East. I was a young man, cocky, strong, and fearless. I was sure of myself and had no doubt that I would beat my opponent. I oozed arrogance. My opponent, on the other hand, was an older man with much more experience. He stood opposite me, bare legs and arms exposed behind a giant, dragon-like mask that covered his face and the trunk of his body. The muscles in his legs rippled underneath his glistening, bronzed skin. He stood there in front of me, calm and poised, waiting for the sound of the starting call. As soon as the gong was struck, my dragon-masked opponent raised his right arm and swiftly landed a harsh blow to the back of my neck. I fell face-first to the ground...and died! There was no hesitation. There was no pain. There was no fuzziness about what had just happened. One minute I was a cocky, self-confident, fearless, invincible young man. The next, I was a lifeless body lying on the packed dirt floor of the arena.

The moment my body fell, my spirit lifted and started floating upward into the sky. I remember feeling completely shocked. This was not supposed to have happened! I was supposed to have won! I was the invincible one! How could this be? I couldn't take in the reality of my death. It so violated my every notion of who I was and how life was supposed to unfold. I was completely undone.

The Great Artist had once again taken his X-Acto knife and ripped through my cherished **Canvas**. And, once again, there I—my former self—stood in front of it, screaming, "NOOO!" I—my current self— was a witness to this **Rupture**.

As I continued to rise above the ground, and in my reeling from the shock of my sudden death, I looked up in front of me and saw the spirit of my opponent rising out of his body as well. Although his Earth body was still in the arena, very much alive and well, the part of his spirit that had "contracted" with me to get this life lesson was rising with me as we both floated above the arena. The rest of him still had work to do on Earth, but this part of him had been there and was continuing to be there—just for me.

I looked over at him, surprised to see that he was coming with me. He looked into my eyes with deep compassion, with a deeper knowing than I had ever experienced. I felt his love for me, his trust in me. He looked to see what I would do with this unexpected ending. When I gazed back into those gentle eyes, my sight broke open and I could see something that had previously been hidden by my unquestionable assumptions. He smiled at me. I smiled back and then we began to laugh. We laughed and laughed and laughed at what I was beginning to see.

At that moment, my newfound realization unfolded in my experience like a vast array of scattered dots suddenly connecting into a picture of exquisite beauty. The recognition of this patterned constellation was immediate and visceral. It bypassed my brain and was not experienced at the level of rational thought or in words. But at that moment, I knew what I knew.

I'll try to put this experience into words. Rising out of his body, my former self's brain was not working with a puzzle, trying to put the pieces together. It was not laboring at untying a tangled knot. Just like Jesus had said in the *Jesus Download Dream*, that process is way too slow and far too painstaking. This was an unmistakable, in-the-moment *knowing*.

In that former lifetime, before my death, I had lived my life thinking that death was the ultimate enemy. Death was the end. Because of this belief, I had spent my whole life proving to myself that I was indestructible. I would not willingly give in to death. It would not get me and snuff me out—not without a fight and not for a very long time, anyway. I unflinchingly believed that death was the end of it all.

In that life, I lived in the **Studio** of The Great Artist Dream. The **Collective Collage**, my additions to it, and most especially my interpretations of all of its images were the totality of my reality. They defined who I believed myself to be and my entire worldview. My determination to stave off death as long as I could was my attempt to make a Procrustean bed out of my **Collage**. In other words, I was going to cram reality into my picture of it, even if it killed me. And it did.

When I actually died and found myself rising above my dead body in the arena, I moved from shocked disbelief and that defiant resisting "NOOO!" to comfort at seeing my opponent with me, to a recognition that life does not end with the death of the body. "Oh, I get it! It isn't that we live and then we die, and that is the end. Now, I see life is an unending series of life/death, life/death, life/death. My body, in that particular incarnation, is dead, but I am alive."

At that recognition, I, as my former self, smiled, then laughed. I laughed and laughed and laughed at my limited sight. And I laughed at the recognition that life was far more loving than I had made it up to be. I no longer needed to run from death. It would never have the final word. What I understood in that pristine moment was that death was always followed by another form of life. I was enfolded in love, and all fear was gone. My opponent had become my teacher and my greatest friend. My death had brought me to a deeper experience of truth and the benevolence of life.

As wonderful as this whole miraculous experience was to witness, my current self, back in Frank's office still needed further clarity about its relation to my neck pain. I went back inside myself and asked my Guides for further clarification. I immediately heard that familiar inner Voice explain:

"*Nancy, you are picking up where he left off. You are feeling the pain that your former self missed with his death. You are the part of the self that is to continue forward from his pain to your next a-ha. In that lifetime, your lesson was: life/death, life/death, life/death. In this lifetime, your lesson is: LifeLifeLifeLife.*"

Wait, what?

Once again, I heard the desecrating R-I-I-I-P of the **Canvas**. I turned in its direction and saw **The Great Artist** standing in front of me, pushing open the flap and asking, "*So, what are you going to do with that, Nancy?*" Once again, I found myself standing on the brink of a wide, open space, but this time eager to see where it would take me.

On the intuitive level, the statement *"In this lifetime, your lesson is: LifeLifeLifeLife"* rang true to me, but its deeper wisdom was still obscure. It was mind-boggling but heart-opening all at the same time. I didn't know what *LifeLifeLifeLife* meant in any rational, much less practical way. It sounded good but the depth of the words lay beyond my reach. All I knew was that I wanted to get the lesson. So, once again, I followed *The Great Artist* into the mystery on the *Back Side of the Canvas*.

* * *

After this second **Rupture**, I began reaching for life wherever I could. Instead of trying to solve my neck pain, I just followed what felt right and true for me in each arising moment. I looked for the spark of life in the world around me.

Surprisingly, one of the places I found that spark was through a regained passion for horses. (I know, who knew?) I had loved horses since I was a young teenager when my friend Joy and I started going out to Almeda Stables on the outskirts of the Houston city limits. We were not trained riders, but back in those days, you could lease a stable horse by the hour. You didn't have to sign any HPPA forms. You didn't have to wear a helmet. You just paid your money and mounted a horse. Once you got into the saddle, you had the freedom to ride all over the open fields. Joy and I loved this. We didn't have any idea of how to really ride a horse—and thankfully, these horses did not require that of us. We just loved the feeling of riding on their backs. We loved the smell of fresh hay in the stable. We loved the spaciousness of the open pastures. After every ride, we would walk through the stables to stroke the forelocks and giant muzzles of the horses in the stalls.

During this time of following the spark, I came across a book called *It's Not About the Horse* by Wyatt Webb (2003). I wish I could remember how I was led to that book. All I know is that it was prophetic. The book is about a form of psychotherapy that incorporates horses into a therapeutic practice called Equine Assisted Psychotherapy. This particular model is structured around a team; clinicians partner with horse experts to do the work. I fell in love with this approach. It opened up a whole new world for me.

I was still living with chronic neck pain at this time, but neck pain or not, I was going to dive back into my fascination with horses and bring them into my psychotherapy practice. Instead of working hard at how to get relief from my pain, I just followed where the spark of life was taking me. And that's exactly what I did. I moved from life to life to life to life, one glimmering white stone at a time.

After completing the certification process, I began offering Equine Assisted Psychotherapy as an adjunct to my private practice. It was an exhilarating and powerful addition, not only to my practice but to my life personally. In 2007, when I was fifty-six years old, I started taking horseback riding lessons for the first time in my life. I loved the feeling of oneness with the horse and the sense of aliveness that reciprocal partnership brought to me. I could feel the equal give and take between the two of us, the mutual listening and responding, the experience of not *two*, but *we*. Learning to partner with a horse taught me lifelong lessons in how to stay in tune. And then somewhere in the middle of all of that partnering, that intentional listening and responding, in the renewed sense of aliveness that it brought into my life, my neck pain simply melted away and has never returned.

* * *

Ruptures are unpredictable by nature. They catch us completely by surprise, shocking us into a new experience of reality—one that on our own we couldn't have imagined. Although this second **Rupture** was preceded by a prolonged experience of chronic pain, both physically and emotionally, this time *The Great Artist*'s slash of the X-Acto knife was not at all painful. In fact, it brought an experience of immediate elation, unlike the heartbreaking shock of my first **Rupture** with my divorce. It exposed a part of my larger worldview that I had not ever really consciously clarified for myself, about the nature of reality itself. This one catapulted me right past the boundaries of time and space, taking my self-concept with it, and when I was brave enough to step through the *Canvas*, I was rewarded with a richer and more whole understanding of what I came here to learn.

QUESTIONS FOR SELF-REFLECTION

1. My first *Rupture* slashed through some very specific personal assumptions about my life, relating to my self-worth and my ideas about love and marriage, while my second *Rupture* focused on aspects of my larger worldview. If you have experienced more than one *Rupture*, did they seem to address different aspects of your life or stay within the same theme?

2. It seems that opening up to all possibilities, even ones that our rational minds don't understand, can be an important portal to new insight. What happens to you viscerally when you think about laying aside all assumptions, both programmed and rational, and moving into a pure, open, creative space?

3. What do you think about the ideas of reincarnation and life lessons? How do your beliefs and experiences shape, affirm, or challenge your worldview? Have any of your *Ruptures* challenged those beliefs? Have they challenged others that are particular to your worldview? What are they?

CHAPTER NINE
UNLIKELY MESSENGERS

The wound is where the Light enters (in).

- Rumi -

This second *Rupture* came in a unique package. It lifted the veil between layers of consciousness, sort of like when, in the middle of a play, an actor steps out of character to talk directly to the audience to give them some insider information. In theatrical parlance, this is called *breaking the fourth wall*. The *fourth wall* refers to the invisible wall that typically separates the actors from their audience. It is what keeps the actor in character. That's what the presentation of this second *Rupture* felt like to me—a peephole into another dimension of reality. A message was delivered to me in this lifetime through witnessing a *Rupture* that was experienced by a former me in a completely foreign lifetime. We don't typically share this multi-dimensional level of communication. The second *Rupture* broke through the invisible wall that usually separates us from other dimensions of the self that live in other times and in other spaces. The more time I spend in the *Space Behind the Canvas*, the more aware I am that the Life-Force is not bound by space or time or any other boundaried experiences of the self. It walks through all walls. It lives by other rules.

In my past life, the **Rupture** came with the sequential experience of life-death-life. What my former self discovered on the **Back Side of the Canvas** was that after the death of his body, a dimension of himself was still very much alive and conscious. That experience shocked him into a qualitatively altered worldview. This life-after-death experience had not been painted on his **Collective Collage**. It lay beyond his pictures of what he believed constituted reality. His death catapulted him into that undefined void that lies in the **Space Behind the Canvas**.

The "me" that I know myself to be in this present lifetime was being shown the unfolding of "his" world-shattering experience. As a witness to it, I was intrigued. I could feel his elation. I laughed with him as he recognized that his death was not the end of himself. A part of him was still very much alive. And I felt the love that surrounded him by not only the inherent Benevolence of the Universe that never lets death have the final word, but also by the spirit of his martial arts opponent who was rising up with him. I was reminded of "I played my part for you."

Witnessing his **Rupture** and the felt sense of love that accompanied it became "my" second **Rupture** through a series of insights. Getting to peek back in time to one of my former self's life lessons did not create the same shock in me as it did in him. He was shocked by the revelations about the nature of life, but for me, it just reinforced some things that I had already believed or experienced as true in my current lifetime—that life always follows death; that we are accompanied by a Benevolent Presence that is actively involved in our continued evolution; that the others who are with us in a particular lifetime do play their parts for us, as we do for them; that often, more often than we are aware, what we believe as true—what we would swear to be true—is just an illusory assumption. These revelations experientially reinforced my previous tentative belief in them. *But that was not all.* My current self's second **Rupture** came with a simultaneous series of other realizations that were brand-new to me in this lifetime. These happened in quick succession. This is so hard to put into words.

1. The first realization was that if we dare to step out of our normal bounds of reality, as I had when a) I decided to ask my pain what it had come to show me, and b) when I chose to possibly find the answer through a past-life regression, I discovered firsthand that those dimensions of reality—an injury and a self in a former life—do exist as unique entities. They have their own level of consciousness, are listening to us, and are eager to communicate with us. I discovered that at least some injuries and illnesses can be message-carriers. I now know it is really important to be genuinely interested in hearing what our health setbacks have to say. Although their outer forms may be painful or debilitating, the messages that they bring can be life-giving. These uncanny experiences outside of our normal way of seeing things provided more direct validation that not only are we not alone in this revolving schoolroom, but we are connected to a Source of Unconditional Love and Divine Wisdom that comes in many guises and is always serving our continued expansion.

2. The second realization was that my recognition of the self as being multi-dimensional—*Maggie*, *Nancy*, the *Soul* accompanied by the *Hungry Ghosts* and *The Great Artist*—was expanded to now include all of my former selves from past lives, as well as all of my future selves yet to incarnate. What is more, each of these aspects of the self supports all the others in their continued evolution. My former self, the martial artist, supported my current evolution by being willing to allow himself to under-

stand that life is always followed by death and that death is always followed by another experience of life. My level of awareness increased by watching him learn his life lesson. And *I* supported *his* process of evolution by being an empathic witness to his life-changing experience, showing how we both played our parts for each other.

3. The third realization for me was that there is something about the self that exists throughout a series of lifetimes and learns as it goes along. Whether literal or metaphorical, these sequential lifetimes are all connected through a series of life lessons that build upon one another. There is an inherent progressive expansion of consciousness that runs like a spiraling thread through multiple lifetimes and multiple identities. What I came to understand is that the **Soul-self** accompanies all the unique versions of ourselves in particular lifetimes. And it is the **Soul** that retains the lessons about the nature of reality through the daily encounters of the unique, incarnated self that we identify with in a given lifetime. This would be my **Nancy-self** in this lifetime.

4. And lastly, the fourth realization that came with this second **Rupture** was what my inner Voice had to say about my current life lesson as *LifeLifeLifeLife*. At the time, I had no idea what it meant, nor could I have predicted getting such a response to my question about my neck pain. It was through the hearing of that unexpected message that I experienced the full shocking effect of my second **Rupture**. The **Canvas** was slashed for a second time, but instead of my **Maggie-self** screaming, "NOOO!" my **Nancy-self** was intrigued, delighted, curious, open, expectant. This **Rupture** altered my identity and my worldview.

It boggled my mind and opened my heart, but it did not scare me or rattle my bones. It came as an unexpected but welcomed surprise.

My mind could not comprehend what this life lesson meant, but I was willing to let it come to me just like Jesus had predicted in the *Jesus Download Dream*: "Your head will be the last to know." What *LifeLifeLifeLife* meant on a practical level was not clear to me at that time, but I didn't need to know. This was just one more shining stone in the moonlight. I picked it up and waited for the next one to glisten in the dark.

QUESTIONS FOR SELF-REFLECTION

1. Have you ever experienced a disease or physical ailment as a message-carrier? If so, what message did it bring? How did you discover the message inside? Do you think it affected your healing at all?

2. Do you relate to the idea that the planet Earth is a schoolroom? How does that affect your reactions and choices as you go about your life?

3. In this chapter, I was surprised by how my past and current selves played their parts for each other. What do you think about having different aspects of the self, in other dimensions of time and space, aiding in each other's expansion?

4. I experienced moving from a casual belief in reincarnation to a lived experience. Have you ever moved from believing in some aspect of reality to actually experiencing it?

5. This second *Rupture* brought to me the experience of a part of the self, my *Soul-self*, that exists through a series of lifetimes. I recognized this aspect of the self as the one who retains all life lessons throughout the whole series of individual lifetimes. Does this resonate with your worldview? Why or why not?

THE THIRD, FOURTH
& FIFTH RUPTURES

CHAPTER TEN

SPLINTERED PIECES

Humpty Dumpty sat on a wall.
Humpty Dumpty had a great fall.
All the King's horses,
And all the King's men
Couldn't put Humpty together again.

- Old English Nursery Rhyme -

During the years I was working with horses and experiencing a new sense of aliveness, a heavy, dark veil fell over my family. The next three **Ruptures**, numbers Three, Four, and Five, all occurred within the last eighteen months of my father's life. And even though they are all related, each one stands out as a distinct mind-blowing, sometimes heart-wrenching, other times heart-opening **Rupture in the Canvas**.

* * *

On an early, hot August morning in 2006, I was awakened by the phone ringing. My mother was on the other end of the line telling me that my dad, who was suffering from cardiovascular dementia, had walked out of their apartment and down the hall of their independent living complex. She asked him where he was going and he said, "I'm going home."

With that declaration, he tripped and fell to the floor and then couldn't get up. My mother couldn't get him up either and the staff at the apartment complex were legally restricted from helping him. So, they called EMS and the firemen, who arrived, lifted Daddy onto a gurney, and then took him to the Emergency Room. After determining that Daddy was not seriously injured from the fall, they still checked him into the hospital for observation. Although he was not physically injured, he couldn't quite hold onto the present reality. He was confused. He wanted to get out of there. His resistance turned into an active rebellion. He started yelling, kicking, and flailing against the nurses' attempts to get him settled. That's when my mother called me. I could hear Daddy hollering out in the background. I asked if she wanted me to talk to him. She said she did and then handed him the phone.

"Nancy, you have got to help me! They're being mean to me. They won't let me up. They won't let me go home. You have to help me!" I could hear the desperation in his voice, his powerlessness.

"I'm coming, Daddy. I'm on my way."

"Yes, yes, get here as fast as you can," he pleaded.

I threw my clothes on, jumped into the car, and drove as fast as I could to the hospital. I parked the car in the multi-level garage closest to the entrance and raced up to his room. By the time I got there, Daddy had been sedated. His hands and feet were tied to the bed railing with durable soft cotton strips. Seeing him in that state broke my heart. I hugged my mom. We stepped outside the room and she explained what happened after the phone call. Daddy had become so combative that the nurses said he would not be able to stay in the regular part of the hospital, and no nursing home would take him in this regressed condition. My father had suddenly become a pitiable Don Quixote fighting at phantom windmills. I can still feel the deep pain of it.

Mom and I were connected with the hospital social worker

who specialized in geriatric care. After reviewing his case, the social worker concluded that our only option was to have Daddy committed to the geriatric psych unit for a psychological assessment and to have his meds regulated. I called both of my sisters and told them about the gravity of the situation, and how suddenly overnight we were locked into the only option left—to have Daddy, our very dignified, brilliant, gracious father, committed without his consent.

Both sisters listened attentively and said that they would agree to any decision that Mom, the social worker, and I decided would be best. A set of legal papers was set in front of my mother asking for her consent to have Daddy committed. My mother asked for each page of legalese to be explained before signing each one, following her attorney-husband's edict: "Carefully read every line of any legal document that you are asked to sign. Never assume what it says. Make sure you understand what you are agreeing to." My sisters and I, like our mother, had carried Daddy's wisdom with us into adulthood. We carried Daddy with us. I watched with full support as my mother gave her permission for my father to be wheeled off to the psych unit.

This whole thing was surreal. It was happening so fast. I couldn't fully stay in my body. I knew at that moment there was no other choice to be made, but since then, I have rethought that decision a million times. Each time, I've searched for some hidden doorway to magically open, but it never has.

It took all day to get Daddy admitted. Once he was ensconced into his new locked-down shelter, Mom and I walked out of the hospital together, each of us shaking, our hearts pounding, tears streaming down our faces. My stomach clenched. My heart ached. We held each other tight before walking off in different directions to get to our separate cars. I found my way back to the covered garage through a daze. I couldn't completely hold myself in space. I was so shocked, traumatized, by the events of the morning, hearing Daddy so desperate and then seeing him so utterly helpless.

When I got to the garage, I had no recollection of where I had left my car. I honestly couldn't remember if I had parked on the entry level or had walked down a set of stairs. My only focus when I drove into the garage that morning was to get to Daddy as fast as I could. I hadn't filed away any outer reminders—the purple, the yellow, the blue floor? So, all I could do was start making my way through the first floor, periodically beeping the remote. I walked around all of the curves of the first floor, clicking the honing device every few steps. There was no return beep of recognition from my car. So, I started walking around the next curve, which led to level two. All I knew to do was keep walking, keep clicking. I started to cry and then sob. I was so lost, so exhausted, so frantic. I was so raw. It felt like I would never get out of there. I felt my father's panic. I was completely overwhelmed and running on fumes. "Help!" my *Maggie-self* silently screamed. All I wanted to do was go home. Like Daddy, I just wanted to go home.

Forty-five minutes later and by the mercy of unseen Angels, I found my car, drove home, and collapsed into bed. I still couldn't tell you what floor my car was on.

The next day, I went to work as usual. Looking back, it's remarkable that I could keep my focus on my clients. My personal world and my professional world were each vying for my allegiance. As my father's daughter, all I wanted to do was sit still, maybe lie on the couch, and watch the clock until I could go back to the hospital to check on Daddy. As a seasoned therapist, however, I had to set aside whatever was going on in my own life and bring my attention to the client in front of me. And truth be told, focusing on someone else helped to make the time pass faster.

I went to see Daddy during the noon-time visiting period. My mother had gone that morning. My sisters joined him that evening. After being escorted past two security checkpoints, I heard the clicking release of the door that led into the lockdown unit. As I stepped through that doorway, I entered into an altered reality. I left the world of familiar patterns and cherished assumptions and entered a space of splintered glass.

Daddy was sitting in his wheelchair next to a round table in the common area. Other patients were scattered around the room. I found a vacant chair and moved it next to Daddy. He looked up at me and smiled in recognition through his medically induced fog. As soon as I sat down, a friendly man sitting across the table offered an unexpected greeting.

"Hey, you!" he exclaimed. "Hey, you! Come over here! What kind of shoes you got, lady?" he asked. "Hey, lady, I got better shoes than that. Come over here." He beckoned, campaigning for my attention like a sideshow barker. His sudden sales pitch exposed remnants of his former life like frayed edges on a well-worn quilt. I simply smiled, nodded in his direction, and returned my attention to Daddy, noticing chocolate icing smeared on the front of his shirt. My stomach clenched. My heart broke again and again. I had to keep reminding myself to remain calm and to just be there with Daddy. "Keep your focus on Daddy."

A moment later, an elderly, disheveled, stained T-shirt-wearing, gray-haired woman came to sit down next to me. "So, what do you think about him?" she inquired, asking my opinion of a man who was not visible to my way of seeing. "Wouldn't you be angry at him if he did that to you?" elevating her voice as she scooted her chair closer to mine, her steely gaze now only inches from the side of my face. Only occasionally glancing in her direction as she talked, I kept my eyes on Daddy.

"I'm madder than hell at him. He got out his Bible and was preaching to me! *He was preaching to me!*" she reiterated with an exaggerated emphasis, exposing the obvious audacity of one who might be asserting her need to have the Bible beat in her direction. "I told him to get the hell out of here!"

She angrily gestured with her hand toward the door. I

turned my gaze toward her to briefly reflect back her feelings, therapist-style. "You're really angry at him, aren't you?" I asked as I tried to join her for a moment, wherever she was.

Sitting in my chair next to Daddy, I became immersed in this new and unsettling milieu. A man trying to sell me shoes; a woman ranting in anger; another one over in the corner, lying back in her adult-sized infant carrier, moaning incessantly as she looked vacantly off into space; a poised, elegant former college professor rearranging the chairs in his classroom, asking us to move from place to place to make room for the other students so they could see the invisible blackboard; and then there was the prim-and-proper, motherly baby boomer yelling obscenities Tourette-style. The woman sitting next to her periodically peeped out from under the blanket covering her head, exposing her reddened eyes and her tear-streaked face. "Come and change me, please," she repeatedly pleaded; "Take me back to my room and change me," clearly indicating that her undergarments were wet and soiled.

And on top of all of this mayhem was a desperate woman standing at the locked unit door, shaking the handle with all her might, screaming at the top of her lungs, "Help me! Help me! Help me! Somebody, get me out of here! Get me out of here!" Her repeated cry provided the backdrop to the whole jangled space, like a loud, heavy metal guitar refrain. I didn't blame her. I wanted out of there too. The only familiar anchor to reality in that disjointed space was the sound of Bob Barker's voice on the TV, hung up in the far corner of the room—"Come on down!" he beckoned. "Come on down!" Bob Barker's voice and Daddy's gentle blue eyes.

The first time I visited my father in the psych ward, my stomach screamed at me as it knotted in response to the adrenaline rushing through my veins. My body reacted as if I had just stepped into some Twilight Zone thriller, except it was worse. This horror show was not a movie. These patients were not actors. This was the real deal. I was actually walking into an altered reality. My skin prickled, my heart raced.

My *Maggie*-emotions leaped and flipped and ran into each other like a cage full of monkeys vying for rungs on a jungle gym. Inside myself, *Maggie* started screaming her time-honored prayer, "Help me! Help me! Help me!" as earnestly as she could. Fear, terror, overwhelm, shock, grief, guilt, helplessness, sadness—deep, deep sadness mirrored my struggling mind, so desperately trying to find a way to put these splintered pieces together into an artful mosaic. There was no connection here between shoes and Bibles, classrooms and moaning, tears, screams and obscenities. The room that held my father was a jumble of thises and thats, fragments of unshared stories. My thoughts raced, hunting for safe ground to land on, trying to make sense of this unbidden collision rendering itself as a major violation to my assumptions of the way life should be unfolding. Inside myself, in concert with the rantings of the mad, was one unwavering, shouting word: NOOO!

"Not this! Not him! Daddy! Daddy! Daddy!" I screamed inside myself.

This was not supposed to be happening to him. "This is not his world! He lives with us! He lives with us in our world!" I found myself once again echoing my father's urgent longing to go home. I wanted to go home too. This was a strange and foreign land. This was some sort of horrible mistake, like some invisible hand had unwittingly plucked my father up and landed him here, as if the transfer orders had gotten all mixed up. The more I resisted the reality of this certain-unreality, the more I pushed away from the acceptance of what was, the more tension and desperation I felt inside.

And then a brief moment of awareness hit me. "Ahhhh!" I recognized that *The Great Artist* had done it again—walked right over to his artist's table, picked up an X-Acto knife, and sliced through my cherished painting of reality, leaving it shredded and jagged, flaccid and lifeless.

"NOOO!" That screaming word bounded in again. "Not this! Not him!"

But it was this. And it was him. Now what? Now what was I supposed to do?

Thirty minutes later, visiting time was over. I gave Daddy a goodbye hug and drove home, crying all the way.

When I got back to the house, I picked up right where I had left off at the psych unit. My *Maggie-self* walked around the house, screaming, "NOOO!" all over again. But, in the background of my mind, Einstein's time-honored, one essential question kept echoing over and over again: *"Is the Universe a friendly place or is it not?"* From where I stood, from what my eyes could see and my ears could hear, the answer to that question was a roaring "NOOO!" All that I could see was a collection of disjointed lost souls. All that I could hear were their fragmented ramblings. Their challenges did not look like benevolence to me. My *Maggie-self* was in full form and I was in full agreement with her. There was no way she was going to move into a space of openness with this one. No way.

However, I was more than that.

Right in the middle of all *Maggie*'s resistance, my **Nancy-self** knew enough to be still and just breathe. This is where my **Nancy-self** once again moved out of the **Foyer** and stepped into the **Studio**. She was paying attention. In the stillness, I noticed that between each resistant "NOOO!" was a gap that was not bound by *Maggie*'s treasured, fear-based assumptions. Somehow, my **Nancy-self** recognized the gap as a portal into the dark, unknown **Space Behind the Canvas**. And so, as **The Great Artist** held the torn **Canvas** open, he asked once again, "So, Nancy, what are you going to do with that?" I chose to follow him and stepped through the **Rupture** once again.

I stopped my protesting, walked over to my computer, sat still, and silently repeated my constant **Nancy**-prayer: "I know nothing. Show me." And then I heard that familiar inner Voice inviting me to listen. Here's what it said:

Nancy, when your answer to Einstein's question, "Is the Universe a friendly place?" is "No, the Universe cannot be trusted to be loving," you will only see what your eyes have been seeing and what your ears have been hearing. You have no other choice but to see the grotesque and to hear the wails of the tortured. And you will be right. From that viewpoint, there is no other conclusion besides "This should not be happening!" But, if you dare to give some space before answering the question, you can make room for more light to come in and more details to be brought to the foreground.

Nancy, look at this. Look more deeply. The situation your father is in is no different from everyone else who lives on the planet Earth. Do you see this? Every one of you is living in your own privately scripted illusion. And when each of you bump into the others whose paths intersect yours, you simply write them into your storyline as each of these is doing here. The only difference is that these stories are more walled-off. There is no sharing of the dreams. In your more normal world, sanity is defined by agreement—collective agreement of where your private stories overlap one another—but does that really make the stories more sane? Does that make them truer than these who do not share that commonality?

You can look at this situation in which you find your father and you can filter it in such a way as to make a case against the Benevolence of the Universe or you can open yourself to seeing something new here. You can open yourself to the Love that is present not only for them, but for you as well...

We would paint another picture here.

The part of your dad that knows the truth, who lived in love and truth and joy and peace—that one who could forgive, who could encourage—the one who was wise and compassionate, who walked with God, with dignity—that one is already gone. He has already surrendered. He had no need to cling. The part that you see here is the remnant of the cloth. It is the part of him that is afraid to let go, too proud to let go, the one who will fight to the bitter end, even though the battle has already been lost. Can you not allow him his dignity in the middle of this seeming hell? Can you not allow him to take his pride to its bitter end? He's undoing it, Nancy. He's in the middle of seeing where it will take him. He's playing out his script the only way any human can play it out, by testing it to see if it will hold him up in the void. He's experimenting to see if he can fool himself and fool everybody else, as well, but just this part of him. Can you give him the time and the space to see where it will lead him? And if not, then what does that tell you about your own scriptwriting and where you look to find your own peace of mind?

Nancy, can you see that this playing it out is not just about your dad playing out the part of himself that continues to answer Einstein's question with a "No"? This situation is inviting you and your mother and your sisters to keep watching how you are answering it as well. Your dad's tenacious holding on to a personally scripted truth that does not reflect the reality of his condition is disturbing enough for you and the others to bring you to the point of surrender as well. It's perfect, Nancy. It could not be more perfect. You just have to have the eyes that see it.

Einstein was right. There is only one essential question to be answered and how you answer it will determine your experience as hell or Heaven, miracle or tragic mistake. Your dad's dementia is in your story, Nancy. Why is this on your plate? That is the question. Instead of looking at your dad and then shouting, "This should not be happening," stop, take a breath, and see if you can be the love you so desperately want to save him and the others. Can you surrender? Can you trust? Can you let go and let it all be perfect just the way it is?

The words from this Voice from the **Back Side of the Canvas** blew my mind and stretched my heart. Those words were so not-me. And yet, they rang so true. The me I knew myself to be literally came to a stop. And that's when the miracle happened.

RUPTURE IN THE CANVAS

Somewhere deep inside myself, I saw that everything I'd experienced in that room—Daddy's dementia, *Maggie-me*, *Nancy-me*, Mama and Betsy and Robyn, the "better-shoes-over-here," the nothings in the air, the chairs that needed to be moved, the Bible and the dirty T-shirt, the "Let me out of here!" railings, and Bob Barker's familiar beckoning call, "Come on down!"—I could see each one of us as a splinter of colored glass falling together in a unique and beautiful pattern like a cosmic kaleidoscope. With each turn of the cylinder—with each jarring turn of events—all the shards of glass shifted into position, relocating in relation to each other. With each rotation, a brand-new harmonious mandala of wholeness effortlessly fell into place, more textured and nuanced, more brilliant and reflective, more inclusive and creative than I could ever have imagined.

My *Soul-self* had emerged.

* * *

The experience of this third *Rupture* exposes the relationship among all the different parts of myself. Even though I had already gone through two previous *Ruptures*, my *Maggie-self* was still alive in me and could be activated at a moment's notice. I am realizing more and more that the *Maggie-self* and the *Hungry Ghosts* don't die off after breakthroughs in consciousness. What evolves is our relationship to them. They are still there in potential form with all their fears, all their doubts and criticisms, all their resistance to where life might lead us. It is up to us to decide whether we identify with them or not. This is why it is so vitally important to develop a stronger sense of self. The *Nancy-self* inside us always carries the power of choice. She is the one who chooses who our authority is at any given moment. She is the one who makes room for the *Soul-self* to step forth.

* * *

My father stayed in the psych unit for three and a half weeks to get his meds regulated. Once he was stabilized, he was moved to a skilled nursing home, where he lived for one more year until his death in July 2007. In the meantime, I would experience two more *Ruptures*.

QUESTIONS FOR SELF-REFLECTION

1. Have you ever had to make a decision that had a great effect on someone else—and then rethought it over and over again?

2. When my dad moved into his decline, my mother, sisters, and I adjusted to it moment by moment. Has your family or group of friends ever had to work together on behalf of another member? Have you ever had to shoulder a crisis by yourself?

3. Once I got a hold of myself, stepped out of my *Maggie-self* and into my decision-making *Nancy-self*, I moved into that space of deep humility and asked for help. This situation with my dad was beyond anything that I could handle or understand on my own. Can you remember a time when you completely surrendered your drive to change something and/or the rightness of your position?

4. When I finally did recognize that I wasn't going to be able to make sense of this situation with my dad, I prayed my *Nancy*-prayer—"I know nothing. Show me." I instantly got a response that blew my mind and opened my heart. That message from the Voice stays with me to this day. I have had to apply it to so many other difficult situations. What kind of reaction did you have to reading about what the Voice said to me? Have you experienced something similar?

CHAPTER ELEVEN
PROMISE MADE

Ask and you shall receive
Seek and you shall find,
Knock and the door will
be opened.

- Jesus, Matthew 7:7 -

While my dad was playing something out in his life, I was playing something out in mine. My Guides took me seriously as I continued to tell them that I knew nothing and needed to be shown what I was missing. They continued to take me to places inside myself that I didn't fully know were there. To explain how all of that unfolded, I'll have to introduce to you one of my dearest friends and colleagues, Jayne Clark. Jayne is gifted in so many ways. In her first career, she was a nationally ranked tennis pro and coach. In her second career, Jayne is a psychic medium, shaman, and life coach.

Now here's how she fits into my story about my dad and me. In 2007, Jayne gathered five other colleagues and me together to practice her intuitive skills in a group setting. In the session, Jayne closed her eyes to the outside world and settled into herself. She allowed her attention to drift toward each person in the room, and when she felt an energetic connection, she would share what she was feeling, what she was intuiting about the person. It was an amazing thing to watch.

When it was my turn, Jayne had a hard time keeping her focus—or, better put, the energy that she picked up on from me would not stay in focus. It kept spreading out in different directions, not holding on to its own integrity. When she told me this, I had an immediate reaction. It reminded me of the worst of my childhood fears. Here I was yearning to have my turn and I kept being overlooked, unnoticed, treated as if I were invisible! Hello, *Maggie*! As the youngest of three sisters, I'd struggled to find my own identity and value. There I was again, catapulted back into the *Foyer* under the influence of the three *Hungry Ghosts*. Seeing me in my distress, *The Great Artist* pushed open the swinging double doors that led to the *Studio* and simply asked, "Ready to come on back?" I once again accepted his invitation and followed him into the larger next room. From there, I gathered myself and asked for Jayne to once again focus on me. With my direct asking, she was able to see me more clearly.

The first thing she noticed was some tension among the members of my family of origin. She said she saw jagged lines drawn between us. She asked if that made sense to me. I told her that my family was going through a really difficult time because my dad was suffering from advanced cardiovascular dementia. We had just moved him into a nursing home after a brief stay in a psychiatric unit. By and large, we had worked incredibly well as a team, each of us allowing the strengths in our personalities to make up for the weaknesses in the others. But there were times when we found ourselves disagreeing, sometimes strongly, on what the next right step would be in caring for this mutually loved man in our life.

Right past the tension, Jayne began to see something else that particularly had to do with me in the middle of all those jagged lines.

"It looks like there is something you need to say, but you are hesitant. Like, I see you walk up to it and then you back off, like you're afraid to say it. Does this make sense to you?"

she asked. "It feels like my jaws are locked," she continued, feeling my hesitancy in her own body.

"Well, I have been very direct with my mother and my sisters about what I think and feel about this whole decision-making process with my dad, so that doesn't seem to fit here."

I was quiet for a moment and then added, "It doesn't feel like there is something I need to say to my dad as much as there is something I need to ask him. I want to hear what he thinks about me, as a separate person from my sisters. I have not ever known if he ever even saw me. I'm wanting to hear that he loves me—Nancy—not just me, the youngest daughter of three."

"Have you ever asked him that?" Jayne continued. "It's like I see you coming up to something and then backing off." she repeats. " Just step into it. Just take that step; don't hold back."

The idea of asking such a question didn't sit well with me. It didn't fit within my picture of how things were supposed to unfold. I just kept thinking that if he really cared about me, loved me, he would naturally come toward me on his own. I wouldn't have to ask him. Asking felt like imposing. It felt like his answer wouldn't count.

I left the session still feeling some anger and frustration about being overlooked by Jayne at the beginning of the session, but also curious about the possibility of outright asking my dad to tell me what he sees and values in me. But, I had no idea how to do it, considering that he was presently living in a nursing home, unable to keep a grasp on the most basic dimensions of reality like time and space.

It so happened that our monthly case consultation group led by Dr. Frank Allen met immediately after Jayne's session in the room next door. Most of us who had come together to help Jayne practice her skills were also in Frank's professional group. So, we all just walked next door to Frank's office. When it was my turn to share in the consultation group, instead of working on a client case, I spilled out all of what I had just experienced with Jayne, unable to contain it.

Frank picked up right where Jayne left off. "But Nancy, could you just ask your dad? What would happen if you asked him?"

"I honestly don't know at this point. I'm not sure if he is even capable of that level of conversation," I responded. "The last time I was with him, he saw his *mother* across the hall, thought we were riding on a train to San Antonio and believed he had spent the night in the library at Texas State University where he went to college. Other times, he's right there with me talking about who's going to win the Democratic nomination or the latest televised golf match," I explained.

"But would it hurt anything to ask?" Frank pushed a little further.

"I guess it wouldn't hurt anything to give it a try. I always bring him lunch on Thursdays. I'll ask him tomorrow. There's really nothing to lose," I reasoned. Despite *Maggie*'s fears, my *Nancy-self* was willing to approach the idea from a space of openness.

Frank smiled and said, "Let me know what happens."

The next day, when I walked into the living room of the nursing home with our takeout lunch, I was hit with the familiar mixture of aromas—the scent of institutional cooking mixed with the pungent smell of urine and the masking springtime scent of a room spray. The coalescence of these fragrances had become expected, familiar. It was just part of all that we had to accept about my father's decline. By that point, my mother, sisters, and I had all adapted to this new arena. However, we could never be completely prepared for which "Daddy" we might encounter when we came to visit. This mystery was unnerving at best and deeply sad at worst. So, I never entered his room without praying.

Ever since receiving that message from the Voice after my first visit to the psych unit that asked me to be the love I so desperately wanted to experience, I started adding a new prayer to my familiar list of two: *Maggie*'s "Help me! Help me! Help me!" and *Nancy*'s "I know nothing. Show me." This new prayer spoken from my *Soul-self* was "Help me to be a conduit of love in this space." So, before entering Daddy's room, I made a practice of silently praying my three prayers. I also started experimenting with sending Daddy unspoken love messages from my heart to his. These messages were not so much verbal as they were energetic. Again, I was experimenting.

On this particular day, I experienced all three parts of myself as I entered Daddy's room with our lunch. I earnestly prayed all three prayers before finding him sitting as expected in his overstuffed recliner, watching TV.

"You hungry?" I asked as I came through the door.

"You bet I am," he said, eagerly awaiting the one last pleasure in his life—the Culver's chocolate malt I'd brought him, along with a cheeseburger.

I fastened his bib around his neck, spread our lunch out on the hospital tray table, cut his cheeseburger in half, wrapped it in a napkin so the bottom wouldn't fall out, and put the straw in his malt. Daddy was still able to feed himself and most of the time could direct the straw to his mouth—in fact, he would get cantankerous if I tried to help too much. I learned to just let him be himself, even when I watched him trying to eat his cookie with a knife and fork or reach for his napkin in the air as if it were floating out in space.

As Daddy enjoyed his cheeseburger, he told me that he was disturbed because he had seen his mother with the man across the hall again and was concerned about how to tell his brothers about it. He wanted to use my cell phone to give them a call and break the news about this indelicate matter. Luckily, I could say that I didn't have their numbers with me. This pacified him for a while, until we moved into talking about how good the malt was and his asking me as he did every Thursday where I got the burger and fries. "Culver's," I would always say. And he would always tell me how he liked that place.

When we finished our lunch and I had thrown all the

trash away, I decided to make my move. I was determined to follow through on my decision, but that didn't mean I felt comfortable about it. The butterflies in my stomach signaled to me that I was about to trespass over a family taboo, or at least what I had always assumed was a family taboo. Before I ventured across that boundary line, I stopped again and asked Spirit to be with me, to guide my words, to help me to be a channel of love in this space.

I took a deep breath and started with, "Daddy, I have a question for you."

This got his attention. He looked right at me with full eye contact—one set of blue eyes to another. "Okay," he said, keeping his gaze on me.

"It's a serious question and it's about me," I continued.

"Okay," he said again, this time with a deepening softness. His eyes, those wonderful Paul Newman eyes of his, softened and intensified all at the same time. I watched in amazement as my dad showed up. There he was. He was back. For a moment, Daddy stepped out of the fog, brought the foot that had already found its roots in the other realm right back into the one that we shared together. Both eyes on me, both feet solidly planted in an encircled space, just with me. I was surprised. I was encouraged to take one more step, myself.

"Daddy, I have always known that you and Mom loved me. I have not ever doubted that."

He nodded.

"But I have not ever known what you thought of me, Nancy—the separate person, called Nancy. I have not ever known what you thought of her, what you saw in her, if you loved *her*—not just as the third daughter."

He nodded in recognition again.

I continued, "So much of our relationship has been indirect. I want to hear from you, not through Mom, what you think of me, what you see in me. Would you be willing to tell me?"

Keeping his eyes focused on mine, he said, "I would love to."

My heart melted like warm butter, no longer able to hold itself solid in the wrapper. And then he proceeded to tell me some things about me that told me he had seen me. He did notice. He did appreciate—deeply appreciated—who I had been and who I had become. He told me how much he appreciated my dedication to helping take care of him and my mother.

I wish I could remember the exact words, but in essence, he said, "Nancy, we trust you. Your mother and I trust that you will be there for us. We no longer hold you as the baby of the family. We rely on you and who you have become."

And then he said something I will never forget: "Nancy, I love you. I have always loved you and I will do anything and go to any distance for you to know that this is true."

I sat in front of him, trying hard to let this declaration in, tears streaming down my face, working so hard to drown out those familiar, cackling, sarcastic, cynical, constantly discounting, life-sucking *Hungry Ghost* voices that taunted, "And this is being said by the same man who just thirty minutes ago thought his mother had taken up with another man and wanted you to call his brothers to let them know? Please!" How quickly the inner saboteurs race in to steal the show, to interpret with their literalism, to discount without a heart.

Yet through all that old, familiar static, I could once again hear the Voice telling me to just be still and breathe, to let my father's words seep into my pores, to let his gaze penetrate my *Soul* without thinking, to just be here in this holy instant.

And for a moment, there we were once again in that ancient space where I became his center and his circumference, and he became mine. It was just Daddy and me encapsulated in a private bubble of him-and-me-ness, no beginning and no end, two notes in a love song called "We," music sailing in like the trail of an ancient shooting star in the dark.

* * *

With that one courageous request, I had dared to walk past all the naysayers, the rule-keepers, past the ones who shake their heads in fear, right past the preachers in their pulpits, their Five Steps to Salvation, past the bigger-than-life **Hungry Ghosts** ready to eat me up. I crawled out of Mama's lap, slid off the rocking chair, kicked off my Buster Brown shoes, and started to climb. I climbed higher and higher, higher than the highest mountains, past the sun and the moon and the Milky Way. Climbed barefoot to the top of the Star of Bethlehem, stood tippy-toe on its highest point, courageously peeped directly into Heaven, and looked straight into the eyes of love. And when I did, I saw my truth reflected back to me.

That's when a tiny voice deep inside who had been quiet for as long as I could remember unabashedly declared, "He sees me! Daddy sees me! He knows me! And he loves me! Daddy loves me." And in my heart of hearts, I knew it to be true.

That was the fourth **Rupture**.

* * *

My father's words were not lost on me. His unveiled presence could not be ignored. I could not pretend that my father had not just made me a promise from the deepest recesses of his heart, even though I didn't know how it could possibly ever be kept.

QUESTIONS FOR SELF-REFLECTION

1. Have you ever struggled to identify and then ask for exactly what you want? If so, what made it so difficult? What have you learned about yourself from that struggle?

2. As I work my way through my *Ruptures*, I am relying more and more on my *Nancy-self* to be an active choice-maker. In this situation, my *Nancy-self* had to quiet *Maggie*'s fears to ask my dad if he truly saw me, separate from my identity as one of his daughters. In what ways has your *Nancy-self* acted boldly on your behalf? In what ways have you reverted to your *Maggie-self* and succumbed to the voices of your *Hungry Ghosts*? (No shame here. We all go back and forth. That's an inevitable part of the process.) If the parts of your programmed self are very different from mine, how have you experienced them and their relationship to each other on the *Back Side of your Canvas*?

3. When my father's dementia limited the normal channels of communication with him, I started experimenting with heart-to-heart messages. Have you ever communicated with someone this way? What has been your experience with it?

4. This chapter exposes how a part of me was still stuck in childhood assumptions about myself, which are based on a deep childhood wound. Can you identify one of your deep childhood wounds? How have you worked with it so far? How does it still affect your life today?

CHAPTER TWELVE

MEMORIAL DAY

Don't believe everything you think.

- Ancient Buddhist Teaching -

On a Monday three weeks after that miraculous connection with Daddy, the nursing home planned a Memorial Day celebration. Mondays and Thursdays were my visitation days, so Mom and I went to join in on the Memorial Day festivities. When we got there, Mom and I found Daddy sitting in his wheelchair on the far side of the nursing station, dozing a little. I walked up in front of him as Mom walked up from behind. "Hey there," I said in greeting.

Daddy looked up at me with an expression of surprise. "Where's your mother and your sister?" he asked in response.

"There's Mama right behind you," I said as Mom bent down to kiss him.

"Oh, I thought Robyn was coming today," he said.

Mom explained that Robyn was at work and that it was Nancy who was going to be with him today.

"Oh, that's fine," he responded as the old, deep childhood pain rushed through my veins. I breathed and returned to center.

"I'm glad to see you and all," he continued, "but I just thought Robyn was coming."

I knew it! He always wanted Robyn more than he wanted

me! That was the real truth, despite anything he had told me a few weeks before. That old toxic feeling welled up inside of me like it had done my entire life.

I sat there once again feeling the sting of the forgotten daughter, watching how my judging mind wanted to take Daddy's confusion and turn it into an arrow to shoot myself with. I kept trying to remind myself about the conversation we'd had in his moment of lucidity. I kept trying to climb back into our bubble of we-ness, to find the Star of Bethlehem again.

I watched as I moved into one framework and then back into the other, watched myself as I wrestled with which one I would hold as truth. I kept reminding myself to breathe and let the feelings go through me and out again. I kept asking Spirit to remind me what love was. And then the **Hungry Ghosts** would raise their ugly heads and I would launch myself back in time to all the family dinners where I watched Daddy engage in conversation with Daughter Number One and Daughter Number Two. Then, back to my prayers. Back to my breath. Back to the openness. Back to trust.

Before long, we made our way with the other residents and their guests to the dining room. A beautiful, big-boned woman with a gorgeous smile and a lovely voice began singing patriotic songs accompanied by her acoustic guitar. Now, in my opinion, a few patriotic songs can go a long way, and the others seemed to agree, based on the stirrings and dozings that accompanied her renditions.

"Daddy wanted Robyn," slipped in again. I felt a deep pain in my heart. "'I'm glad you're here and all, but I thought Robyn was coming.'" That phrase kept repeating in my mind. My stomach clenched into an old familiar knot and I launched into my prayers: "Help me! Help me! Help me! I know nothing. Show me... Help me to be a conduit of love in this space."

It wasn't long before Daddy thought we were waiting in line to board a train again, assuming we were about to embark on some sort of travel adventure. All through "God Bless America,"

"America the Beautiful," and even "The Eyes of Texas," Daddy was busying himself and me by taking off his Velcroed sneakers and asking not-so-subtly when the barbecue would start. "*Bluebonnets...bluebonnets...*" the entertainer sang, commemorating our great state of Texas. I heard the Velcro rip and Daddy's shoe hit the floor for the third time.

A time or two, he surprised us with his sense of humor, which was remarkably balanced and patient in the middle of what was becoming an obvious organizational failure. I noticed a little smile creep across Daddy's face. I asked him what he was thinking about.

"I just keep wondering what a fella needs to do around here to get a dog and a bag of chips," he answered. But then he left us again and tried to inch his wheelchair up closer to the "passenger" in front of him to make his way to the train station.

"*Everybody clap now... Ev-ery bo-dy!*" The Social Director beckoned to the napping crowd. She swayed her ample hips in time to the patriotic tunes. Mom and I exchanged more than a few glances, rolling our eyes at each other, wondering when we were ever going to get our food, particularly because it was getting harder and harder to keep Daddy occupied. I felt like I was trying to handle a circus monkey with a mind of his own—or at least part of one.

When the last song finally ended, the promised dogs and chips were served. We ate with gratitude and then wheeled Daddy back to his room to take his nap. I had been so preoccupied with the never-ending singing and Daddy's altered reality that I had momentarily lived in a space of peace, but the **Hungry Ghosts** struck up again as I walked back to my car.

He really wanted Robyn there, you know. Did you really believe what he said the other day? Think about it. If he had truly valued you when you were growing up, he would have looked in your direction. He would have asked you about your day. And he wouldn't have been looking for Robyn right over your shoulder this morning. Come on!

I know I am not alone in this struggle.

* * *

That Memorial Day celebration would stay in my memory as a reflection of an inner battleground between opposing inner voices inside myself, each competing for my allegiance.

The taunting voices coming back so soon after my breakthrough conversation with Daddy left me hopeless and wondering if they would taunt me forever. From my little girl's perspective, I had assumed that all I needed to feel at peace was for Daddy to tell me that he saw me and knew me, valued me as a separate person in my own right. That's what had been missing. And so that's what would bring me into wholeness. Or so I thought.

His declaration of love for me brought a temporary relief—an elation. I had accepted it as a miracle. And on one level, it *was* a miracle. Daddy did come out of the fog to meet me eye to eye, heart to heart. I couldn't deny that that had happened. But the effects of that miracle moment were too soon overtaken by the assumptions I'd carried since childhood, under the influence of the powerful **Hungry Ghosts** who were not convinced.

It continues to surprise me when I am able or am brought back to a place of true inner peace or joy or deep connection and then, moments or days or weeks later, find myself right back in the **Foyer**, trapped in the snares of the inner saboteurs ready to swallow me up. What is up with that? How can that be? Have I not done any real work? Have I not evolved at all? Will this never end? I get these questions from my clients all the time too. This process of personal transformation is a frustrating ordeal. It spirals around and around, returning us to our childhood wounding—not to torture us, but to give us another chance for it to be healed, another chance to see it differently.

* * *

Let me make something clearer. The day of the miracle between me and Daddy was real. We genuinely connected on the level of the heart. He did temporarily step out of his dementia to meet me in an important moment. That in itself was a great act of love, unlimited by time or space or mental capacity. His words, so tender, so appreciative, so acknowledging of what he had noticed and valued in me, were real too. And then, that final declaration, "I love you, Nancy. And I will do whatever it takes and go to any distance for you to know that that is true." Well, it doesn't get any clearer or better than that.

Then how could I have reverted into the *Foyer* so quickly? There are several reasons for that. One is called *ego backlash*. This often happens after we accept *The Great Artist*'s invitation into the *Studio* or bravely step through a *Rupture*. The *Hungry Ghosts* are threatened when we pull our allegiance away from them. This is the very thing they defend against most. They want to stay in control because they think this will protect us from further wounding. They are the parts of the self that are blocked from love. They are the parts that don't believe it is real. And so, for us to trust in love and boldly step out of the *Foyer* or through a *Rupture* leaves them scrambling, sort of like how a mother reacts when her child is about to run into the street.

If we are in a vulnerable state, ego backlash can easily pull us back into its orbit. If we are feeling stronger inside ourselves, ego backlash can bring us back to a choice point. My *Hungry Ghosts* did this by asking, "Are you sure that Daddy really values you? Do you really want to hold onto that? You're going to get hurt by getting your hopes up again, you know."

When those old voices ask us those old questions, if we make them conscious instead of just letting them buzz around in the background somewhere, we can stop and ask ourselves, "Is that true? Is that old, taunting voice speaking the truth?" And this gives us a chance to consciously answer their questions, rather than unconsciously react from the childhood position. This process is like exercising a muscle. Every time we ignore those taunting voices and take a step on our own, that muscle gets stronger. The result is that we stay centered longer and we don't get hoodwinked so often.

The childhood wound gets healed in layers, and it's amazing how many layers there are. As I understand it, the wound is finally fully healed when we have reached a level of full identity with love and we cease our struggle to find it. I'm not there yet. The spiraling process continues until all of our blocks to love's presence finally go *poof!*

It's important to remember that the wound is never what factually happened to us. As a reminder, the childhood wound is a combination of mistaken assumptions that we have labeled as true. It is always what we made up about what happened to us. It's about the meanings we attached to it. Because Daddy quit looking in my direction after my grandmother's brain surgery, because I observed he was no longer as delighted with me when he got home from work, *I made it up* that must mean I was not worthy of his attention. I didn't have enough of *something* to spark his interest. And Betsy and Robyn clearly did. I watched his look of pride toward Betsy and his look of joy toward Robyn. From my experience, I got no look at all. It makes sense that I would turn that against myself. I wasn't able to consider all the extenuating circumstances my family was dealing with during my childhood, so I assumed his lack of interest was a reflection of me.

The wound wasn't that my father's behavior changed; it was my blaming myself and my perceived inadequacies in the face of it. Wounds like that get imprinted into our psychic hard drive. They can't be erased. Every time we click into that archive, the same primordial childhood video plays like an old TV rerun. What triggers the replay is something in the present that is reminiscent of what happened in the past. Most of the time when that happens, we unconsciously click on the frozen-in-time memory and step inside of it like entering a movie. And, when we step inside of it, it feels just like it did the first time around. This is our default position. It's where we will end up if we don't stop and consciously think about it.

It's where we go when we forget we have a choice.

In that sense, the childhood wound that hurts so badly can be seen as also *playing its part for us*. This part gives me chills. It's all so brilliant and so perfect. The **Hungry Ghosts** use our wounding against us to reinforce the childhood assumptions, which makes us feel terrible. But they also provide us with a chance to choose love instead. Love requires conscious participation. The pain from the wound then acts as an alarm bell to signal that we have unconsciously moved away from connection, from truth, from that which brings us back to life. It provides us with the opportunity to get to choose for ourselves how we want to respond. Unconditional love does not intrude. It waits to be invited. Making the conscious choice to move back into truth, into love, into the experience of life is the greatest privilege we have as humans. From that perspective, the pain from the wound becomes the portal back into Divine Wisdom, Unconditional Love, the Life-Spark. It plays its part for us.

Important to note: Sometimes when we stop and consciously choose love, we are immediately brought back into its presence. Sometimes, however, we don't feel any different. We still feel terrible. No worries. It is not our job to know how to get ourselves back into connection. *It is simply our job to choose to be brought there.* We do this by first admitting that we don't know how to get ourselves back into alignment with love, and then by asking to be taken there. "I know nothing. Show me." And we will be shown. It is not our job to predict how or when. Our job is to ask and then to have the faith the size of a mustard seed that we have been heard.

QUESTIONS FOR SELF-REFLECTION

1. This chapter exposes how falling back into our old childhood assumptions about ourselves is our default position. In other words, we will automatically live out of those assumptions unless we consciously choose to ask to be led out of them. Can you identify with that frustrating process of going back and forth between your **Maggie-self** and your **Soul-self**? What kind of situations trigger that dynamic for you?

2. When my dad was surprised to see me instead of Robyn, I got a knot in my stomach. His desire for Robyn triggered memories of all five of us sitting at the dinner table, with Daddy's gaze fixed on Robyn— and my feeling ignored. Can you recall a recent experience when you felt an old, familiar stab to the stomach? What were the circumstances? Could you attach any memory to it?

3. At the end of this chapter, I move into my therapist's position to describe my understanding of the paradoxical role a re-triggered wound can play in our lives. We most often identify with the pain of a revisited wound, but paradoxically, it's playing its part in our healing, too. Can you see this happening with your childhood wounds in your own life?

4. Once again, prayer was a vital part of my Memorial Day experience. Reflect, once more on the role that prayer plays in your life. Has it evolved as a result of any of your **Ruptures**? In what way?

CHAPTER THIRTEEN
PROMISE KEPT

*For, as has been given, it is not
all of life to live, nor yet all
of death to die. For life and death
are one, and only those who will consider
the experience as one may come
to understand or comprehend what
peace indeed means.*

- Edgar Cayce -

Over the two months following the Memorial Day fiasco, the temperature rose close to a hundred degrees and Daddy began to make a steady decline. He quit drinking his malts on Thursdays and became increasingly belligerent with the workers who tried to help him with his basic needs. We continued to meet with the nursing home and hospice staff to adjust his treatment to fit his devolving situation. We were being forced to make the kinds of decisions that nobody ever thought they would have to make, like choosing between his safety and his freedom. "Do we start strapping him in his wheelchair to prevent his continued falling or do we let him attempt to walk even though he is sure to fall again?" We opted for freedom, always trying to make decisions that would continue to eke out the last threads of self-empowerment.

My father had become so, so feeble—feeble in body and in mind. It was incredibly hard to watch his attempts at mental clarity or any kind of self-propelled movement. And in the middle of all that, amazingly, he still responded to life as if he were in control. Once a mighty lion, now just a mouse of a self, but a mouse with a ferocious squeak.

One Friday in mid-July, during a full staff meeting, we were told that Daddy would in all likelihood continue to live for at least three more months. Although there were no signs of a final decline, we had asked that direct, uncomfortable question in the face of making yet another decision on his behalf—"Can you tell us how much longer?" His current nursing home was going to increase their rent by $500 per month. Angst over finances was a constant in the mix of other concerns about the quality of his care. We were considering moving him to another nursing home, this one just a block from Mom's apartment. Though reputable, it was less expensive and less modern. We were torn between protecting our parents' nest egg and maintaining a sense of familiarity, given Daddy's mental state. Constantly finding ourselves trying to predict the future, we wished for a crystal ball, prophetic clues emerging through the tea leaves, but neither one appeared, so we were left with our collective best judgment.

On the following Monday, Mom called a private family meeting with my sisters and me to once again discuss our options. Uncharacteristically, she began the meeting with, "I want to start this meeting with a prayer. I want each one of us to take a turn."

We all joined hands in agreement, although we were not at all accustomed to praying together like this. Mom began with something like, "Dear Lord, we ask for Your guidance as we continue to make decisions for Roy's care. Please help us to feel Your presence. Help us to hear Your will for him. But if we can ask for what we want and what we think would be best for him, we would ask, Lord, that You take him. Take him in his sleep tonight, ease his suffering, take away his pain, and let him simply go to sleep and be with You. We surrender to Your will, Lord, not our own. In Jesus's name, we pray."

My sisters and I followed in turn. We were not as bold as our mother in asking that he be taken that night; we focused our prayers on being guided on our next step in the decision-making process and asked that we be brought to a deeper level of trust in the benevolence of the unfolding events. Yet inside, we each shared our mother's more direct request. We were all running short on our ability to watch such a slow, resistant end of life.

After the prayer, we again each took turns sharing what we thought about moving Daddy. We were all open to it, so a few days later we decided to go back and visit the alternative nursing home one more time. We were impressed, and we made plans to move him on the first of August. We felt at peace with the decision. We could all exhale. Again.

Within minutes of our leaving the prospective nursing home, I got a call from the hospice nurse, informing me that Daddy had started refusing to take his medication and was no longer eating. The nursing staff had been watching him closely and this change had literally happened overnight. The hospice nurse made it clear that this looked like the beginning of the end. They would continue to monitor him, but all moving plans were put on hold.

I went to see Daddy that afternoon. He recognized me but was very quiet. Despite my mother's prayer, Daddy went to sleep that night but awoke the next morning, still not eating, not taking his medication but willing to drink a little juice. I went back to see him that next day and got him to take a few sips of water. He was conscious but kept his eyes closed most of the time and looked startled when I tried to talk to him. I let him rest and sent him blessings from my heart to his.

That night I went to sleep as usual but was awakened by a startling dream. It was short and to the point:

I found myself traveling down a country dirt road. To either side of me was a thick forest of tall, dense trees. All of a sudden and coming from the right, a big, black horse pulled out into the road in front of me. He was bridled with long reins that extended behind him. He stopped directly in front of me and turned his head to look in my direction. He stood still and simply looked at me with his soulful, knowing brown eyes. And although I could not see it, I knew that he was pulling a cart with a coffin inside.

I woke up and checked the clock. It was 5:04 A.M. Was this an omen? Had Daddy just died? The phone did not ring. I went back to sleep. I realized later that the dream had been very literal. The coffin was there, ready, being slowly pulled into full view. But for the moment it was just out of sight.

On Wednesday afternoon, the hospice nurse called to say that this was definitely the end. He suggested that we let all the family members know this was the time for a last visit. All the grandkids that lived in town took turns coming in to see their "Pappy," to tell him that they loved him, one last time. After the grandkids left, the rest of us sat around Daddy's bed, telling Daddy stories and stroking his legs or his arms, taking turns putting a damp washcloth on his fevered forehead.

Daddy's body shook with tremors, agitation, and discomfort. We watched and soothed, eagerly awaiting the morphine that had been ordered. Over the next few hours, Daddy slipped into a deeper sleep and his breathing became more labored. I found myself wanting to keep a hand on him. I just needed to stay in touch. Daddy would inhale, hold his breath. I would watch and wonder, "Is this the last? Is he choosing to go with this one?" But every time, he would find a way to release what he had taken in.

As I watched my father struggle, the memory of my experience in my vision of an Asian arena came into mind. I remembered the feeling I'd had as the young, virile martial artist when I suddenly became aware that I had died and yet was still alive. I remembered how good it felt to float up out of my body and how fun it was to experience that life lesson: life-death-life-death. I remembered laughing and laughing and laughing. So, with each struggling breath, I sent Daddy silent messages of encouragement. "There it is, Daddy. Right there. Just keep on going. It's okay. You'll like it. It's fun. I've done it... When you see the way out, take it and keep going."

Again, I was experimenting. I didn't have any roadmaps to follow on this one. I was just living on the *Back Side of the Canvas* in a space of openness.

Each time, despite my encouragement, Daddy found the strength to keep his spirit and body intact. Inwardly, I would smile and trust in his timing.

* * *

By 10:00 P.M., Mom was exhausted and we told her to go home and get some rest so she could be there again in the morning. She reluctantly agreed. The nurse on duty had told us that the timing of this sort of thing could not be pinpointed, but judging by his breathing and his vital signs, it would be at least hours, if not days until the final breath. By 11:00, we decided to divide up the next forty-eight hours into shifts. Betsy would spend the first night at the nursing home, promising to call if there was any change. Robyn, her husband, John, and I all drove home to get some rest before returning the next morning. I went home, took a shower, and dried my hair, but left it flying in every direction. At about midnight, once again trusting in that open space on the *Back Side of the Canvas*, I crawled under the covers and sent a final heart message to Daddy before I went to sleep.

"I'm not sure how all this works, Daddy, but if it is possible for you to come and see me on your way out, I would love that. Now, don't scare me or anything; it's not like I want to see a ghost in my room. But if you could find a way to come and see me one last time, I would so appreciate it. If, on the other hand, you just want to keep on going, then go on. I don't want to interrupt your journey. I love you, Daddy." I sent my message like I had been doing during our visits in the nursing home from my heart to his, and then went to bed.

Once again, I was awakened in the night, this time by the feeling of anxiety at remembering my father was dying. It was as if, while I was sleeping, I could temporarily forget. I woke up, thinking, "Oh yeah, Daddy is dying..." and then, with my eyes still closed...I *saw him*! There he was in front of me, looking a little younger than his eighty-nine-year-old self, those kind, deep blue eyes looking directly at me again, penetrating my heart.

He smiled slightly, delightedly, saying, "I love you, sweetheart." He kept his gaze on me.

"I love you too, Daddy," I said, thrilled that he was there.

Then an amazing, somewhat ineffable thing happened. All of a sudden, we simultaneously began to review our relationship. It is as if we became one mind. We both looked down and saw the timeline of our lives together. And as we moved from year to year, we could both feel the gap that kept us apart. In recognition of this gap, at the very same instant, we both paused to say, "I'm sorry. I'm sorry for the part I played in keeping us apart." But then just as suddenly, we both stopped ourselves, each of us realizing that to apologize for the gap would be a dishonoring of the deeper truth of our relationship. There in that moment, we saw it. We saw the truth. Underneath the gap, all around the gap, filling in the space of the gap, we loved each other. There was no doubt about it. There was no question. We knew it and we felt it. The simple truth was that we loved each other, and had all along. We looked into each other's eyes and smiled. We were one mind. We were one heart. No gaps, only love—an open space of shared love, once again encapsulated in a bubble of we-ness, but this time it somehow included everything and everybody. Nothing was left out. There were no gaps, anywhere.

And then, this part was kind of funny. All of a sudden, in the background I heard some music playing. It was a song I had heard on a commercial on TV.

"*I'm free...to do what I want...any old time... I'm free...to do what I want...any old time... I'm free...*"

And with that final background declaration, Daddy was gone. I opened my eyes and looked at the clock. It was 3:43 A.M. I was in shock. I was elated. There was so much flooding in all at once. The only thing I knew to do was get up and get dressed. I didn't think about it. I just did it. As soon as I brushed my teeth, the phone rang. It was Betsy.

"Nancy, I just wanted to call and let you know that Daddy just died. I've called Robyn and Mom. They are on their way up to the nursing home. He's still in his room. Why don't you come on over?"

"I know!" I exclaimed. "He just came to see me! I just saw him! He came to tell me he loves me! I'm putting my clothes on right now. I'll be right there."

I threw on my clothes, put my wild hair in a ponytail, and headed for the nursing home. I had just heard that my dad had died, but I was anything but sad. I was in pure *joy*.

When I got to the nursing home, Mom was there, and Robyn and John arrived a few minutes later. We all gathered around Daddy's bed again. We touched him, spoke our last words softly, privately. After some time, we decided to go sit in the living room area down the hall. As we moved in that direction, Patricia, the nurse who had been with Daddy when he took his last breath, stopped us in the hall and said, "Well, all I know is...I don't know where your dad went, but at about 3:45 this morning, he was out visiting somebody. There must have been something really important for him to do because his vitals were normal at that moment and then he just left."

"It was 3:43," I heard myself say in my dazed amazement. "He was visiting me. And the something he had to say was important to me."

"Well, I believe it," Patricia said, as if I had just told her that I had a turkey sandwich for lunch.

* * *

That spring, I dared to ask my father if he loved me as Nancy, not just as his third daughter. He answered me with a promise: "I love you, Nancy—always have, always will. And I will do whatever it takes and go to any distance for you to know that that is true."

And lo and behold, on July 19 at 3:43 in the morning, he did just that.

That visitation was my fifth *Rupture*.

This one took me further past the edges of the *Canvas* than any of my previous *Ruptures*. It took me right past all previously held definitions of time and space, life and death. It took me into a space of love and connection and communication that bypassed all of those presumed boundaries. It took me into a space of love that included everyone and everything, not just me and Daddy. It took me to a place of pure transcendence, where life lives right through death.

Oh, my gosh! There it was: *LifeLifeLifeLife*.

QUESTIONS FOR SELF-REFLECTION

1. Have you had a personal experience with a loved one going through a slow decline? Who was it and what was that like for you?

2. A few days before Daddy died, I had a prophetic dream of a horse-drawn cart carrying a coffin. Have you ever had a prophetic dream? If so, what was its message? Or do you have a hard time believing in such a thing?

3. When my family and I gathered around my father as he was dying, I silently sent him heart messages like I had done the whole time he was in the nursing home. But I also silently encouraged him to go ahead and let go, telling him that I had done it before and that he would like it. How do you respond to this kind of experiment with energetic communication? Have you ever had such an experience? What brought it about and did it leave any lasting effects on your life?

4. I experimented one more time with sending Daddy a request, again heart-to-heart, right before I went to bed the night he was dying. This is another example of my *Nancy-self* willingly stepping past the boundary of the *Canvas* on her own, without *The Great Artist* having to rip through it. Have you experienced anything similar during or just after a *Rupture*? If you are in the middle of a *Rupture* right now, can you think of ways that your rational mind might be hindering you?

5. Have you ever experienced a visitation from someone who has passed? What was that experience like for you? How did it affect you at the time and how has it affected your life or your worldview?

A DEEPER LOOK #2

CHAPTER FOURTEEN
FORGIVENESS

*Forgiveness is still and quietly does nothing.
It offends no aspect of reality, nor seeks
to twist it to appearances it likes...*

*Do nothing then, and let forgiveness show you
what to do through Him Who is
your Guide.*

- A Course in Miracles
The Foundation for Inner Peace -

I am stepping out of the linear narrative again, like I did between *Ruptures* One and Two, to give you an insider's perspective on a cherished moment—a moment that, for me, came as the unexpected gift of forgiveness. Its position between the section describing *Ruptures* Three, Four, and Five and the detailing of *Rupture* Six is not at random. This chapter not only takes us deeper into this cherished moment but also serves as a bridge between these two sections, exposing the inextricable connection between those two corresponding eras of my life. *Ruptures* Three, Four, and Five are all about the healing of my relationship with my father, while *Rupture* Six describes the start of a relationship with my destined Soulmate. Yet, since all *Ruptures* are intricately tied to our self-image and programmed beliefs, this experience of forgiveness also spirals us back to my very first *Rupture*: the devastating recognition of my first marriage as duplicitous.

The final destination of forgiveness described in this chapter could not have happened before my father's departing visitation. *Rupture* Six could not have happened before I was able to forgive both myself and my former husband for all that transpired through our unconscious connection. Each phase of my life opens the way to the ones that follow, starting back at the very beginning.

From where I stand now, some thirty years after the first *Rupture*, I can see a thread that runs from that initial heartbreaking event all the way to its closure, to its full healing. But that's only the visible part of the journey. So much of the evolution took place underneath the surface of my awareness. It is only from where I stand now that I can see that it took a series of events, everything before and after the first *Rupture*, for this long-awaited healing to manifest. I see today that there is some unseen Force, some unseen Benevolent Force that has been propelling me to see more and more of what the *Hungry Ghosts* blocked from my awareness. Just like the full-grown oak tree that lives inside the acorn, there is a natural pathway secreted inside our *Souls* that is hard-wired to move us toward wholeness. Looking back, I can see the telltale signs of this built-in, invisible force that has always been working on my behalf, consistently pointing in the direction of the greater truth. On some deep and mysterious level, I can now see that every encounter in my life is tangentially connected to every other. Every event, every person, every opening into awareness that preceded this healing has played its part in its ultimate emergence.

It is only from this teleological perspective that I can see healing is synonymous with the expansion of consciousness, with moving into alignment with love. Healing is the experiential recognition of the real truth, of reality as it is, not as we assume it or desperately want it to be. Paradoxically, healing does not mean repairing the **Rupture in the Canvas**. No, it is the emergence of the perspective that has the eyes to see through the gaping hole into the Love-filled space behind it.

The healing of my first **Rupture** came to me through the gift of forgiveness many years after the fact. I don't believe that forgiveness could have emerged without allowing my father's true love for me to be experienced firsthand. His visitation on his way out was not an isolated, miraculous event. Instead, it was the healing of all that had come before it, which played its part in opening the way for greater love to come in. It's important to note that the ultimate level of forgiveness described here took years in the making and came as an unexpected gift. I didn't do it. I couldn't make it happen. It emerged through the aid of hidden, healing Forces. As was foretold in the *Jesus Download Dream*, my head was the last to know. To explain, we have to circle back around to that very first **Rupture**.

* * *

Finding out the truth about my first marriage was my first heartbreaking, mind-boggling, life-changing event that slashed right through my cherished **Canvas**. The shock of it shattered all I thought was real and valuable about love and marriage, as well as who I believed myself to be. Finally allowing that hidden truth to break through into my awareness proved to be only a tiny peephole into an ever-widening evolution of consciousness that followed. Lifting the veil of denial around my first marriage was by far the most devastating. It shook me to my core. As such, it has taken years of soul-searching therapy, dedicated self-reflection, mindful meditation, and moving into deep humility through praying **Nancy**'s constant "I know nothing. Show me" to get me to a place of grace around it.

Underneath all the outer changes and adjustments I made after my divorce—finding my way on my own, launching each one of the kids, starting a new private practice, having mystical visions and dreams, rekindling my love of horses, sending heart-to-heart messages to my father—another part of me was busy waking up to a deeper level of truth.

Although I am going to describe that process as a linear progression, trust me—it was anything but straight and smooth. Evolution does not move from A to B to C; it moves forward in fits and spurts. Yet when we observe it closely, we see that the overall movement is one of a gradual expansion. And, although it might not seem like it at the time, it's worth every painful, humiliating, and freeing moment.

I was devastated by the idea that the man I was married to could bald-faced lie to me, that he could carry on a double life right under my nose. Realizing that shocked me, terrified me, deeply saddened me. It infuriated me. In those early stages of my awakening to the truth of my marriage, I saw Josh as the Grand Deceiver. He might as well have had pronged horns and a pitchfork. According to my newly but limited enlightened perspective, Josh was the bad guy here—the very, very bad guy. And all I wanted him to do was grovel. At first, that's all I could see.

And on one level, admittedly, Josh was the villain. He *had* lied and he *had* lived a double life for years. He *had* betrayed me and whenever I questioned him about any of my suspicions, he would inevitably turn the conversation around and blame me for my self-righteous, judgmental ways. That was not merely a projection on my part. And so, for me to finally feel some justified anger at him and to call him out on it without backing down or apologizing was a step toward truth, a step toward healing. It had to happen.

But there was so much more. I know now that what truly caused the **Rupture** was *what I assumed Josh's behaviors must mean about me*. Although the form was very different, my unconscious *Imago* marriage to Josh was a full-blown reenactment of my worst fears from my childhood.

If Daddy didn't look in my direction, if he showed no interest in me, if his attention was always on those other females—Betsy or Robyn or Mom—or those other important things out there in the world, that must mean that I was not as equally interesting enough to hold his attention. I wasn't lovable enough for him to want to spend time with me. For some reason I couldn't quite name, *I* wasn't enough.

Josh played out in real time my worst fears about myself, which were primarily based on my relationship with my father. If Josh kept wanting to be with other women, if he kept wanting to travel further and further out into the world, clearly it meant that I was not enough for him. He needed much more. He appreciated me for being the steady home base for all of us. He appreciated my dedication to our children. And to his great credit, he generously supported me and paid for all of my and our children's continued education. But he did not appreciate who I was as a unique person in my own right. He wasn't much interested in what I, Nancy, had to offer. And that was just like my experience with my dad. If the two men that I loved most in the world were just not that into me, what must that say about me? Through Josh, I now had proof of what I had always suspected must be true: I must not be valuable or lovable enough, period.

When I allowed that misguided but seemingly logical conclusion to finally hit, it was like a stab to the heart. I felt completely alone and worthless. And to make matters worse, if Josh could enroll that many women, some of whom were my friends, to join him in his disregard of me, I must really be deserving of being treated as if I didn't exist. Josh turned my worst childhood fears into a present reality. My most dreaded fear was true all along. And that horrifying conclusion about my worth was part of what kept me in denial for so long.

I was not only my father's daughter, however. I was also my mother's. And if you remember, my mother grew Angel wings when her mother became incapacitated. She modeled giving to the one in need and also the one in power. The message I got from my mother was that love means to give and give and give, no matter what. This was driven home even more strongly by *The Church*. I learned young that love means always putting the other person first. Love means self-sacrifice. And besides that, women should always be subservient to men.

You might also recall that after my grandmother's surgery, in her grief, my mother held me close to her in our antique rocker. She held me tight as she silently sobbed. As a toddler, I took in her sorrow and held it inside myself as if it were mine. I thought that was what she was asking of me. My mother needed me to join her in her pain, to absorb it for her. And that's when I learned to be still and quiet and good because our family couldn't handle another full-blown personality. From the time I was two, I had been programmed to go invisible, to deny myself for everyone else, to be very, very good and still and quiet, to be a holding space for everyone else.

And that's another reason I stayed under Josh's spell for so long. I truly believed that he was right to be angry with me. Inside myself, my *Hungry Ghosts* agreed with him. They kept telling me to not do anything to make him angry or to leave me. They kept telling me that I didn't have the right to disagree with him, to hold onto my truth if it contradicted his. They kept telling me to ignore all of my alarm bells, to let him have his way, to compromise myself, to absorb his truth as if it were mine, to be still and quiet and good. And so that's exactly what I did for twenty-one years.

When I finally did let the truth in and allowed it to be exactly as it was, I went into shock. Not only was I ripped to pieces, but I felt completely duped by life. In my mind, I couldn't have tried any harder to be more loving. I couldn't have tried any harder to be good, to do what was right, to be the wife and mother I had been trained to be. And it didn't work. That's what was so shocking! I felt like I was the brunt of some cruel cosmic joke. Everything I believed to be true about love and marriage, everything I believed to be true

RUPTURE IN THE CANVAS

about me and my role in life, everything I believed to be true about my whole identity was shattered when the real truth of my marriage came barreling through. With that first **Rupture**, the only "me" I knew myself to be was exposed as just a painting on a **Canvas**. And she was ripped to shreds.

* * *

Of all of my **Ruptures**, that first one was the most vicious in exposing the depth of my entrenchment in my childhood programming. Allowing the truth to finally come into my awareness collapsed the most formative underpinnings of my identity and exposed so many of my rock-solid assumptions about life and love as stories that I had innocently adopted as true.

It has taken years to fully understand the unconscious dynamic that trapped Josh and me together. And, as Harville Hendrix has so clearly detailed through his life's work, this dynamic is not exclusive to the two of us.

According to Hendrix's theory on romantic relationships, when we go out looking for our partner, we unconsciously put out feelers for someone who seems to be the perfect answer to our need and desire for love. This *Imago* partner appears to fill in the gaps where each individual believes her/himself to be lacking. We assume that, unlike our parents, this partner will love us more unconditionally and will reflect our value more clearly. We get to finally have what we always wanted as a child, and this newfound partner is the one who will fulfill it. It is this assumption that dooms the *Imago* relationship to fail.

Unconsciously caught in this dynamic, I began to gradually realize that Josh, my cherished partner whom I believed would finally fill my **Soul** and ease my pain was, in fact, not. And that is when I began to try harder and harder to get him to play the role I had scripted for him. This is a common and predictable part of the *Imago* dilemma. Sadly, most of us do not give up on our increased effort easily. Most of us have to play out the push and pull, the hopes and the frustrations, the power struggles and tug-of-wars inherent in that kind of unconsciously, co-created, symbiotic relationship. Over time, the tension back and forth usually increases the polarized positions and each partner becomes a caricature of him or herself, feeling needier and more desperate than ever. Josh and I both played out this torturous insanity in full unconscious fervor.

From where I stand now, I recognize that Josh did not cause me to step back and hide. He did not cause me to deny my rightful place as a full human being. His use of intimidation did not make me his victim and his being with other women was not the source of my being betrayed. I brought all of that with me into the marriage from what I assumed to be true from my childhood experience. Josh played out what I believed I deserved. His criticisms and disregard of me expressed out loud and in real time what I was secretly most afraid must be true.

Likewise, neither did I cause Josh to use his anger to intimidate me. My self-consciousness over his accumulating wealth, my urge to hold him back from his wanting more and more out of life did not cause him to stray. My confronting him about being with other women didn't cause him to lie. He brought those ways of dealing with the stresses of life with him into the marriage. All of those are his learned forms of self-protection. In some way that I could never fully know, my outward actions toward him must have reflected his worst fears about himself as well. I'm not sure what the specifics of his worst fears were, but I am quite certain that the way I showed up in our marriage triggered his programmed childhood reactions. We were both acting out of fear and insecurity and blaming the other for it.

Let me quickly add here again that this does not mean Josh didn't lie, intimidate, violate his vows, or treat me as if I was expendable. He did all of that. Nor does it mean that I didn't shrink back from life, play the victim, try to force Josh to conform to my ideals, or micromanage my affection toward him. I did all of those things. But doing all of those things was not the cause of our conflict or our pain. Not recognizing our own inner demons or honoring the depth of our childhood wounding was what caused all of that mutual suffering.

* * *

Once our unconscious ways of self-protection get exposed to the light, once we recognize them as hidden parts of ourselves, we can stop blaming the other for our pain. We can take ownership for our part in the power struggle and we can finally bring compassion to the parts of ourselves that unwaveringly believed in our misguided assumptions. Once we get that far, forgiveness is a natural outcome. Opening our hearts to all the messiness of being human replaces the need to blame. We all live in very fragile glass houses. And when we finally realize that, we are set free.

* * *

Confession: I kept a record of everything that happened between Josh and me, starting with my journal from the Spirit Quest. I kept every letter and note that we wrote to each other, expressing all of our feelings—everything. All of the love letters that we wrote back and forth during our separation and all of the angry, blaming ones too. I kept a copy of the letter that I wrote to the other women letting them know that I did exist and that their being with Josh was not limited to just the two of them. I kept all of the letters that I received back from the handful of other women who responded, as well—some defensive, some genuinely contrite, some asking for forgiveness, others confessing they had no idea he was married.

I kept the letters that I sent to my family members when I fell apart and the ones they wrote back. I kept notes of encouragement and support from my friends and extended family, letting me know that I was not alone. I kept my notes from my therapy sessions and all of the notes from my visits with my divorce attorney.

I kept all of that in a box labeled "*DIVORCE*" that I stashed on a shelf in my garage. A part of me wanted to keep a written record to prove what had happened, to validate the devastation of it all—and, truth be told, at first, to validate my innocence in all of it. There was something really important about that box. Keeping it felt like a genuine honoring of the part of me that had experienced the explosion, the complete loss of identity, the debilitating trauma. Both my wounded *Maggie-self* and my self-determined *Nancy-self* kept that box in place.

It's not like I went out to the garage and read any of it that often. No, it was enough to just know that it was there. The DIVORCE box held the reality of the pain in place. And for the longest time, that was important. Over the years, while I was uncovering my hidden layers and connecting them back to my childhood, I would imagine myself going out to the garage and finally shredding all of its incriminating, validating evidence—but I couldn't. I just couldn't. Something would always stop me. To permanently destroy it felt like betraying the part of me that had experienced it. I didn't want to make light of what *she* had gone through, of where her experience had taken me. I wanted to honor that watershed rite of passage. And so, for years and years, probably as many as sixteen, I kept that DIVORCE box safely in place on its shelf in the garage.

And then one day—not on any particular day, but one day after my father's promised visitation—I walked out to the garage, took the box off the shelf, walked to the outdoor grill, lit a stack of charcoal, and started feeding all the saved documents, all the letters written back and forth, all of it, piece by piece into the rising, alchemical flames. I watched as the bits of charred paper rose with the breeze. I watched as they floated out into the open sky. And as they floated free, so did

I. My ***Nancy-self*** is the part of me that decided to continue to listen to her evolving experience of truth. She's the one who struck the match. And when she did, my ***Soul-self*** was released.

Coda

I want to press pause here and, just like at the end of a movie when the credits are running, the scriptwriter prints a blurb on the screen that gives the movie-goer some additional information about each of the characters. I realize I have left you clueless about what happened to Josh after our divorce was final. I shared so much of what happened to me in the years that followed, it's not fair to leave him back there in his forties. He hasn't remained frozen in time any more than I have.

Although I don't really know him that well anymore, and I don't presume to know the details of his inner journey, I can tell you that he has maintained an ongoing loving relationship with all of the kids and, now, the grandkids. They all still go out to his lake house in the summers. He still spends hours pulling them behind the boat on skis or one of those giant inner tubes. He loves to take them on exotic trips.

I know he stopped drinking years ago. Maybe most important to note is that Josh married the true love of his life some five or six years after we divorced. I believe him to be devoted to her. From all outward appearances, she shares his vision of "spectacular" in a way that I could never do. She readily joined him in his quest to make the world his oyster. And over the last twenty-something years, they have done just that.

I will always be grateful to Josh for playing his very difficult part in our *Imago* relationship. Had we not wrangled with each other as tenaciously as we did, neither of us would ever have been able to arrive where we are today—both of us in a deeper, truer experience of love.

QUESTIONS FOR SELF-REFLECTION

1. Go up high and look down on the timeline of your life. What do you see from that vantage point? Can you see a thread running through it? How would you describe the theme or set of themes embedded in that thread?

2. Have you ever been fully forgiven by someone else? How did that come about? How did it feel at the time? What did you learn from it?

3. Have you ever fully forgiven someone? How did that come about? Was it from trying really hard or choosing to be the bigger person? Maybe deciding that what they did wasn't that bad after all—or did it evolve into your awareness over time like it did in mine?

4. Is there something from your past that still feels unfinished? Unhealed? Unforgiven? Is there a metaphorical box in your garage? What does it feel like you need to do to feel at peace with it?

THE SIXTH RUPTURE

CHAPTER FIFTEEN

THE LITTLE SECRET

*Your soulmate will be
the stranger you recognize.*

- R. H. Sin -

I have explained a little bit about what I experienced as a single person after my divorce, but I have not shared the whole story. I am circling back around now to fill in some of the gaps. It took years for me to find a new equilibrium and I needed every one of them. If I had known what lay ahead of me when I stepped through that torn *Canvas* for the first time, I might not have ventured forth at all. But that's the whole point. We never know what lies beyond the destruction of the *Canvas*. It's always a surprise. Although I didn't know it at the time, that pivotal decision allowed room for dormant parts of myself to emerge and take life. It opened the door for my destiny to come alive.

    Those early years of living on my own were tumultuous. I lived with a constant knot in my stomach. I felt out of my element. At first, the only thing that kept me going was knowing I had to support my kids, both emotionally and financially. Over time, however, life did begin to calm down. The kids left home one by one, I began to find my groove with my career, and over time, I started falling in love with my independent life. I liked living on my own time, eating what I wanted to eat, going where I wanted to go without having to consider anyone else. This was totally new for me and I found the freedom in it exhilarating. Those years of living on my own—me living with just me—were an essential part of my evolution. This was me living more from my *Nancy-self* and less from my *Maggie-self*. That progression, from erratic to equilibrium to exhilarating, is what I experienced consciously. It was an evolving process.

Down beneath my level of awareness, however, it's as if a seed pod popped open, spilling out a collection of tiny seeds into inner fertile soil. Over the seventeen years that I was single, the seeds began to germinate. First, they sent their hairlike roots deep into the dark soil. Then one by one they shot up tiny green sprouts that broke through the surface and into my conscious awareness and experience. One sprout was my kids leaving home, the next was the maturation of my career. The healing of my relationship with my father was another one. Experiencing and learning to trust in my Guides was a recurring one. And that takes us to the theme of this chapter: another seed was my love life.

After the devastation of my divorce, I put all notions of *men* to sleep. There was too much else happening and the mere thought of seeking out romance made me hurt all over. I kept the lid on that jar screwed on tight for years! However, there finally came a time in my exhilarating single life with myself when I began to long to share it with someone—the *right* someone. Yet there was a caveat to this longing: I definitely did not want to have to date. I felt positively clear about those two realizations but wasn't quite sure how I was going to bring them together. How do you jump from living life on your own to partnering without going through the dating scene? Ironically, that's kind of what I did.

First confession—I did sign on to one of those online dating sites for a short while. I stretched myself well beyond my comfort zone, posted a profile, and uploaded my staged photo in the designated box. And then, before I knew it, messaging back and forth became a part-time job. On occasion, I would meet up with the guy, have coffee, lunch, or (rarely) dinner. And that would usually be the end of it. Though I was proud of myself for having jumped out there and putting myself on the line, I hated every minute of it! So, that phase didn't last very long and solidified my conviction that I really didn't want to date.

Second confession: If what I am about to share did not expose the wonders of the Universe, I would be way too embarrassed to put it on the page. After all, I could keep it a little secret just between me and myself because not one other person ever witnessed it. And I sure didn't tell anybody about it. But this embarrassing part of the story is vital to the whole thing. So, here it is.

I lose track of the exact timing of all of this, but let's say about fourteen or fifteen years into living on my own because I wasn't dating on the weekends, I started watching a steady diet of Meg Ryan movies. (I realize I am aging myself here again.) I got caught up in the routine of watching and rewatching and rewatching over and over again the classics—*When Harry Met Sally, Sleepless in Seattle, You've Got Mail.* There was something in these guileless romantic comedies that touched something in me that I couldn't explain even to myself. The whole thing doesn't make any rational sense. But the something that touched me in these movies was a repeated theme: Two unsuspecting people meet in an unusual way, where life sort of brings them together without their orchestrating it. And—drumroll, please—they fall in love without ever formally dating.

On any given Saturday night, I would watch the chosen Meg movie, feeling a deep inner ache as I projected myself into the Meg Ryan role, only to have the movie come to an end. Inevitably, right after Harry finally kisses Sally under the rotating disco ball, or Annie meets Sam at the top of the Empire State Building, or Kathleen Kelly and Joe Fox meet up in the rose garden, I would realize Meg had gotten her guy again and

I was still sitting there on my living room couch with a hankie in my hand. It would be right about then I would realize that I, Nancy, *not* Meg Ryan, was still sitting at home alone and the clock was continuing to tick me right past my prime. While I was single, I went through menopause and started losing my hair. Crow's feet sprouted talons around my eyes and I began developing jowls along my jawline. Pa...leeze!

So, my post-menopausal self would wipe her eyes again, blow her nose again, and then pray to her invisible Angels again. "I don't get it! What am I missing? Just tell me! I feel so stuck! Give me clarity and then give me the courage to act on that clarity. It feels like I'm supposed to have a partner again, like I'm going to be married again, but he's not here! What am I missing? Who am I missing? Nothing's happening!"

And then—and this was consistent—a name would flash into my mind. It would sneak in like a whisper, sort of like a little secret, and then rush off again because I wasn't supposed to hear it or own it or allow for it to even enter in. *"Dave... Dave Bair..."* the Voice would say. Every time, in response to this name, even though I knew it was right, I would say out loud in my living room, "It can't be Dave Bair! I've told you a million times, it can't be Dave Bair. He's a former client!"

And so, the Voice's "Dave Bair" response was always summarily dismissed. End of discussion. Door locked. Not going there. Amen. That is, until the next Saturday night, when there I would be again, eating my Lean Cuisine and watching Meg all over the TV screen, again—–Meg staying all cute and perky while my hormones were drying up.

* * *

So, okay, who is this Dave Bair?

Dave and I met in the Sunday school class taught by Dr. Bob Lively where I met my friend Suzanne. At least, *Dave* remembers meeting me in Bob's class, though truthfully, I don't remember meeting him. When Bob was out of town, he would often ask me to teach his class, so Dave knew who I was long before I knew who he was. I remember meeting Dave the first day he came in to see me as a new client.

I will never forget walking into my waiting room and seeing Dave: a really good-looking man with crisp white hair and the bluest of blue eyes, who stood up to greet me with a warm smile. When our eyes met, I felt a shiver run through my body and I heard the Voice say, "He is the masculine version of you. He is your male counterpart." It was as if I recognized him. I was shocked and delighted in the strangest kind of way, but I didn't skip a beat. After all, I was an experienced therapist. I had been practicing the unflappable "blank-slate" presence of my profession for years. So, I quickly tabled that inner Voice and stuck out my hand to introduce myself before showing this Dave person back to my office.

After that first session, I saw Dave pretty regularly as a client for the next year and a half and a sprinkling of times throughout the next few years. About four years after our first therapy session, Dave joined the *Course in Miracles* spiritual study group I was leading. He was in that group for the next five years.

It was right in the middle of those five years that I began to run into Dave Bair everywhere. I have not run into anyone else on the planet as many times as I randomly ran into Dave— at three different local grocery stores, a golf course parking lot, walking my dog, at two different lectures at opposite ends of town, and in the shoe department at Nordstrom's.

The reason I tucked that little "he's your male counterpart" comment far away into a dark corner of my mind, without intending to ever pull it out and examine it, is because, at that time, the professional ethics guidelines under the laws of Texas stated that a therapist could not ever have any kind of romantic relationship with either a current or former client— *not ever*. (That period has now been reduced to a minimum of five years according to the LPC Licensing Board of the State of Texas and down to two years according to the American Psychological Association.) At that time in my life, if I was anything, I was ethical. I had been taught to follow the rules, so that's what I did to the letter of the law. Hello, **Maggie**.

Sitting across from each other in our *Course* group enabled me to get to know Dave on the level of the heart, but it prevented me from knowing all of the basic details about his life. I didn't know the kinds of things that come out in the first weeks and months of a typical dating relationship. Like, I didn't know the identifying characteristics of his brothers or his sister, how they ranged from an iconoclast artist to a straight-up, party-line Republican. I didn't know that when he was in elementary school he made Christmas tree forts in the backyard every year, or that he had been an acolyte—a candle lighter—in the Episcopal Church, or that he started throwing newspapers from his bicycle when he was fourteen, drove his 1952 Rambler into the garage door because the brakes didn't work, and re-stacked the fallen bricks to make it look like it hadn't happened.

I didn't know anything about his college years—that he and his best friends all moved to Berkley in the early 70s to experience the rising anti-establishment counterculture firsthand. I didn't know he had been the Executive Chef at the Shoreline Grill next to the Four Seasons in downtown Austin, or that he hated sushi and loved chicken enchiladas with tomatillo sauce, just like I did.

What I did know is that he teared up anytime he felt touched by something, just like I did, and hated it as much as I did. What I did know is that I had grown to love him for that tenderness. And instead of it making him look weak, which is what he feared most, it made my knees turn into Jell-O and my heart dance a little jig.

Dave and I sat across from each other in that *Course* group sharing all of that mystical, heartfelt, connected-to-Spirit reality for five friggin' years. We both presented ourselves with perfect decorum the entire time. We stayed on topic. We never physically touched in any way—I hugged other group members, but never Dave. We certainly never intentionally met outside the group, and each of the aforementioned chance encounters was brief and held tightly within professional boundaries. But, despite all of that propriety, I was beginning to fall in love with this man. I convinced myself that secretly falling in love with him was not the same thing as having a personal relationship with him out there in the world.

I kept my feelings for Dave snugly sealed away in a compartment all its own because that is what kept the *Hungry Ghosts* from eating me alive and my hand-painted *Collage* safely intact. It's what kept *Maggie* from freaking out.

QUESTIONS FOR SELF-REFLECTION

1. Do you believe in love at first sight? In Soulmates? What has been your experience with falling in love?

2. One of the mysteries of the Universe is the phenomenon of coincidence or synchronicity. In my life, randomly running into Dave Bair occurred far more times than could be predicted by statistics. How do you explain this? Have you experienced anything similar?

3. Another mystery was my continuing to hear an inner Voice, who responded to my repeated question about who my Soulmate might be, with the repeated answer, "Dave Bair." I repeatedly dismissed it, thinking that I knew better than it did. What is your experience with getting an intuitive hit on something? Did you ever act on one? Did you ever override one like I did?

4. Were you surprised to see my *Maggie-self* take over after all I had experienced on the *Back Side of the Canvas*? Have you ever witnessed yourself doing the same? What does this tell you about the process of psychological/spiritual evolution?

CHAPTER SIXTEEN
THE CHOICE

You are never upset for the reason you think...
There is only one problem;
choosing fear over love.

- A Course in Miracles
The Foundation for Inner Peace -

Something unexpected happened in one of the *Course* group meetings in the spring of 2010.

Steve, one of our group members, suggested that we all attend a concert at a new music venue out in the Texas Hill Country, called the Blue Rock. He thought it would be an incredible experience for us to share as a group. He labeled the whole affair as a spiritual experience—the natural beauty of the space, the generosity of the hosts, and the gifts of the artists all contributed. He was animated in his description. Though our Course group had never met socially before, Steve suggested that we might consider it a kind of "spiritual field trip." Dave, who had also been to the Blue Rock, seconded his suggestion.

Steve looked in my direction to get my response. I was kind of taken aback. Meeting outside the bounds of my office had not ever occurred to me before, not even for the *Course* group. I posed the question to the group and everyone else was in favor of our joining in this adventure together, so I agreed.

With this decision, I once again dismissed the *Hungry Ghosts* who were warning me to stay clear of this idea and walked into the *Studio*. Magical things happen in that space.

There was an added layer to this process that I need to mention. During the last two years of the *Course* group, I was also a member of a psychic group. This group was formed by a colleague of mine, Cindy Myska, who can close her eyes and see words running across the inside of her mind as if they are being typed on a computer screen. Yes, wow! When her sister Donna closes her eyes, she sees images that give her symbolic information. The third member of the group is one of my dearest friends and colleagues, Jayne, whom you met in Chapter Eleven. Jayne is both a medium and a psychic. I would say I have a deep intuitive connection, but these women are the real deal. I was grateful to be playing in such rich and deep waters with all of them.

The purpose of the psychic group was to provide us with an opportunity to practice our psychic/intuitive skills. It was really fun and I loved it! For me, the group gave me a chance to move into that liminal space I have talked about in previous chapters, a space that is neither literal nor imaginary, that holds a reservoir of sacred wisdom. Most of the time when I choose to access that space, I am either in a very stuck place or I am terrified about something. The psychic group allowed me to practice tapping into that wisdom from a neutral but curious space.

As it happened, our psychic group met on the same day but several hours before the Blue Rock field trip. Cindy introduced the new task for the session: each of us was asked to think of a question on a topic about which we would like more information. We were to hold the question silently in our minds while another member tried to intuit information that might be helpful.

The exercise seemed like the perfect way to get guidance about my situation with Dave. I could ask for help without having to say anything out loud. I didn't want to have to tell the group that I had fallen in love with a former client! That felt shameful, disgraceful. To *Maggie*, this whole field trip situation was terrifying! The rest of me was all a-twitter. I was in major conflict. My stomach clenched. My heart pounded with both excitement and excruciating angst. I could hear the *Bookkeeper's* incessant clacking in the background.

When it was my turn to silently think of a question, several came to mind. "What am I to do with my feelings toward Dave? What is the truth? Am I supposed to violate my professional ethics to be with this guy?" I had been paired with Donna, who knew nothing about my turmoil and knew very little about me personally. As I held my questions in mind, I held my breath in concert.

Donna closed her eyes and immediately said, "Oh, I am getting, 'Yes, yes, yes!' very emphatically. I don't know if that is yes to three different questions or a strong declarative in response to one." Then she said, "I see you sitting in a chair and a man is standing behind you. He is tall with dark hair. He is kind of dressed like my husband did in the 70s. And oh, your ex-husband just came in. He's standing next to you. Now, I am seeing your dad. Oh, he's so proud of you. He loves you so much. He is saying, 'You will know what to do and you will do it.'"

I felt a warmth spread through my body with Daddy's appearance. I felt his support.

"Now I am hearing trumpets playing! This is crazy!" Donna exclaimed with obvious surprise.

"Uh ...it feels like we aren't supposed to be talking about this. This is about a man... You don't want to talk about it." And then she stopped, opened her eyes, and asked me, "Does this make any sense to you?"

I quickly responded, "Yes, it does, but for me to explain it to you, I am going to have to tell you the question. I was hoping I wouldn't have to do that." It was clear that I wasn't going to get clarity by having this thing continue to spin around and around in my own head. I needed a more objective perspective than my own. So, my *Nancy-self* ventured forth.

"It *is* about a man. And, no, I am not having an affair or anything, but here goes. The truth is I am secretly in love with a former client, who isn't my client anymore but is now in the *Course* group I lead." As I said it, I felt myself cringe. "Nothing has happened between us. I have kept impeccable professional boundaries, but this is up for me today because the *Course* group is going to the Blue Rock music venue tonight as a kind of spiritual field trip. It will be the first time that we have been anywhere together outside my office. I am a nervous wreck. My question was, 'What am I to do about my feelings toward Dave? What is the truth? Am I supposed to violate my professional ethics for us to be together?'"

My anxiety spiked and I felt torn inside. The ever-present caustic taunting from the *Hungry Ghosts* surrounded me with their deadening energy as the familiar sound of the *Bookkeeper*'s calculator continued to clack perceptively in the background. *Maggie* was once again caught under their spell, but that was not all. I could also feel my *Nancy-self* getting excited about spilling the truth into the room. She was so tired of holding it in. She was so tired of being good. I was torn between wanting to get it all out in the open and keeping it locked up tight.

Cindy jumped straight into the messages from Donna. She leaned forward in her chair and focused her gaze on me.

"So, Nancy, who is the man standing behind you?"

"It sounds like Luther, my sister's husband who passed away."

"What is significant to you about Luther?"

"I think it's the last message I sent him when he was dying. It said, 'When I look to the past, I feel sad. When I look to the future, I feel afraid. I am loving you in every present moment.' It feels like Luther is sending the message back. In essence, he is saying, 'Stay in the present moment. That's where love is. Love is in the present moment.'"

"Now, Nancy, what did you learn from your marriage to Josh?"

"To trust in the Holy Spirit and the truth of my own experience. Don't live out of old beliefs or outer rules. I can trust my truth."

"Okay, so what are the trumpets?"

"In the *Course* group today, Dave asked, 'Why does it have to be this hard? Why can't God just knock down all the walls for us?' And I replied, 'Oh, that reminds me of the story of the Israelites marching around the walls of Jericho, blowing their trumpets. The walls didn't fall because of the sound of the trumpets. The walls fell because the Israelites believed that God would make them fall. They blew their trumpets to signal the strength of their belief and trust in His power. This story tells us if we put our faith in God's ability to knock down all the walls, they will fall. Our task is to believe and trust, not to work hard at knocking them down on our own.' The sound of the trumpets is telling me to have faith that God will knock down the barriers that are in front of me. My job is to believe in that."

"So, Nancy," Cindy said, looking me in the eye, "where is all of this taking you? Can you move forward with this? Can you at least put your toe over the line?"

"I still can't!" I blurted out. "I can't unless I get a clear sign from Spirit that I am to move forward."

Donna broke in, "Nancy, your brother-in-law is coming in to see you. Your dad and even your former husband...you have trumpets blowing, for Heaven's sake! What more do you need?!"

At this, we all laughed. I had indeed gotten several clear signs. I saw that. I felt the truth in all of the messages. And I knew on some level, **The Great Artist** was inviting me to claim my space in the **Studio** more boldly. I was being given the opportunity to use my free will to get clear about what I really wanted. Opening the door to the possibility of a real relationship with Dave terrified me. It would mean violating my professional code of ethics. It could lead to lots of criticism. I could potentially lose my license. But my worst fear was the possibility of hurting Dave, of hurting our *Course* group, of any of them feeling overwhelmed or betrayed by me, feeling that I was no longer trustworthy. I felt torn in half. Equal pressure in both directions between my fear-based, rule-keeping *Maggie-self* and the deeper truth of my being. There was so much at risk, or so it seemed. And it was my *Nancy-self*'s job to make that choice.

By the end of the psychic group, I felt myself open to the possibility of somehow approaching Dave. The messages that I got from all the family members that came into Donna's inner vision, the sound of the trumpets, and the meanings attached to each of these transmissions were enough for me to loosen my grip a tiny bit. As my *Maggie-self* remained in the *Foyer*, my *Nancy-self* stood firmly in the *Studio*, ready to step once again into "I know nothing. Show me."

I left the group in a daze. I still felt myself pulled in two directions at once. I knew on some level that the decision I was grappling with was not really about whether to approach Dave. The real choice facing my *Nancy-self* was about which of the other two parts of me, *Maggie* or my *Soul-self*, represented the deepest expression of my truth. I had to decide which part was me and which part was an imposter. Backed by the *Hungry Ghosts* in the *Foyer*, my *Maggie-self* held firm to her learned belief in living by the rules, but I couldn't deny that my *Soul-self* left the psychic group that day feeling the spark of a tiny ember glowing deep inside my heart. It was up to me, my *Nancy-self*, to either fan it into a flame or let it die out.

QUESTIONS FOR SELF-REFLECTION

1. Do you think of yourself as intuitive? Why or why not?

2. Donna's intuitive reading exposes the realm of knowing that speaks in images rather than in words, like the dreams and visions I have shared with you throughout this book. Have you had any personal experience with symbolic intuition? If so, describe.

3. In this chapter, I share my continued struggle with the tension between honoring a rule or living out of my personal experience of the truth. What types of life situations trigger your old, fear-based patterns?

4. When my *Nancy-self* finally decided to gingerly move into that space of openness by telling my psychic group what I was struggling with, new and unpredictable options opened up for me. Are there moments in your life when you consciously decided to let go of a set of assumptions that you had previously believed was sacrosanct? If so, what was your experience following that decision?

CHAPTER SEVENTEEN

IN AND OUT OF THE BOX

*And the day came when the risk of
remaining tight in the bud
was more painful than the risk
it was to bloom.*

- Anaïs Nin -

After leaving the psychic group, I spent the afternoon doing mindless tasks, trying to make the time go faster. At about 5:00, I got in my car and started following the directions I'd printed out for the Blue Rock since this was before any of us started relying on GPS. When I got to a T at the end of the highway, I wasn't sure which way to turn, so I pulled over to reread the directions. I heard a car pull up beside me, and there he was again, that Dave Bair, in another chance encounter. I felt a shiver run through me, just like it had the first time I met him in the waiting room nine years earlier. We both rolled down our windows. Dave smiled as he asked, "Are you lost? Want to follow me in?"

"Yes," I said, "That would be great."

I followed Dave as he eased back onto the highway and then down a series of winding country roads that finally led through a rock-bordered entrance with a sign on it that read *"Blue Rock."* Parked cars lined the granite gravel driveway that led up to the house. Dave parked at the end of the line and I pulled up next to him. When we got out of our cars, Steve was there with his mom, who was not a part of our group. After introductions, the four of us walked together through the live oaks up to the house, cicadas singing out their familiar, rhythmic cadence.

As it turned out, none of the rest of the group came that night! It was just me and Dave, and Steve and his mom. So much for a group spiritual experience. Alrighty, then. With fewer people to buffer my proximity to Dave, I felt my blood pressure rise. My heart raced. I had a knot in my stomach. These sensations continued to signal both my terror and my thrill. I kept praying inside myself, "Oh, God, help me! Please help me! Tell me what I'm supposed to do!"

Dave went ahead to save us some seats while the rest of us took a few minutes to enjoy the natural beauty outdoors. The back of the property was set up high above a deep ravine. It opened into a vast, panoramic vista. Rolling hills covered in scrub oaks and cedars stretched in every direction. At the base of the ravine was a winding stream and in the middle of it sat a huge boulder which took on a dusty blue tint in the angled light of the western sky.

Steve was right. There was something magical about this place. We were hushed into a sacred silence as the sun began to slowly sink toward the horizon, painting overlapping layers of violet and pink and orange. Just for a moment, the anxiety running through my body oozed down through my legs and feet, rooting me deeply into the earth.

The spell was broken, however, when we heard the sound of a bell signaling it was time to come in and find our seats. Rows and rows of chairs were set up in the center of the crowded concert room. Dave was waving to us at the end of an aisle. We waved back. Steve and his mom filed into the row ahead of me. The only seat left was, of course, next to Dave! He stepped into the aisle so I could scoot in between his seat and Steve's.

The great room was cavernous in size but warmed through

its natural stone fireplace and rough-hewn pine floors. Huge windows and French doors flanked both sides of the room, bringing the beauty of the surroundings inside, creating the aura of a natural cathedral.

Eliza Gilkyson, known for her soulful, contemporary folk music, was the featured artist for the evening. As an Austin-based musician and songwriter, Gilkyson is no stranger to Texas audiences. Although I knew of her, I couldn't have named any of her songs or hummed any of the melodies, but I was drawn in immediately. The uniqueness of her voice, her genuine, unabashed, just is-who-she-is-presence had me with "Howdy!"

Due to the tight seating arrangement, Dave and I sat closer to each other than we had in any other setting. He always sat across from me in the *Course* group. It was as if we were two magnets, sitting there next to each other, being both attracted and repelled by the closeness, a raw desire mediated by restricted assumptions and habits of mind. I felt torn between a wildly screaming "yes" and a prohibitive, solid "no."

Gilkyson's music made the torture even worse. After her first honky-tonk he-done-me-wrong opening, it was as if each subsequent song was written just for us, for Dave and me. Her words seemed prophetic and made my heart ache. She sang her classic, *He Waits for Me* about her deep longing for her man, and his for her, the flaming passion that ran through her veins. The woman was killing me!

Dave remained silent and attentive during Eliza's performance. I hoped that his heart was aching with every romantic phrase just like mine was, but he showed no outward signs of his inner experience—no accidental touching, no leaning in my direction, no catching my eye. I was left in the mystery. It was torturous!

Halfway through her performance, Eliza brought the concert to a pause. Everyone got up to stretch their legs or go in search of refreshments. Dave and I walked out together, following the crowd. After a cookie or two, he mentioned that the stairway on the other side of the kitchen led to a lookout tower. I asked if he could take me there and soon found myself following him up the winding staircase, which opened onto a 360-degree landing bordered by a cedar and hog-wire railing. By this time in the evening, there was just enough light in the early summer sky to expose the surrounding hill country, which stretched for miles in every direction. Dave asked, "How'd you like to have your coffee up here every morning?" We were both caught in the beauty of the moment, but we maintained our physical distance of propriety in one of the most romantic spots on the planet. I felt like an awkward sixteen-year-old being chaperoned by invisible hall monitors. The *Hungry Ghosts* in my head once again seized the moment to get a firmer foothold.

After we made our way back to our seats, Eliza picked up where she left off, singing her soulful love ballads, searing a red-hot iron into my heart. She ended the evening with two of her most sacred songs, starting with *Requiem*, a prayer for the mercy of Mother Mary, for the blessed Mother to make the path clear through her Holy light, to carry us in her gentle embrace.

"Yes, yes! That's it! I cried out inside. "Light my path...quiet my fears...Mother Mary, have mercy on me!"

And then came *Sanctuary*, a prayer of gratitude for Divine presence. That's exactly how I felt – grateful. Even though I was terrified to have such strong feelings for Dave, even though I was so confused about what to do with those feelings, I could not deny that I also knew that I was not alone. I was being heard. I was being guided. I was being held.

Everyone in the audience sat in hushed silence, all of us realizing we had just been ushered into an otherworldly space of sacred union. No one wanted to move or speak or leave our seats. We all just sat there, not wanting to break the mystic spell.

We did eventually get up and walk back to our cars. The rhythmic cadence of the cicadas had been replaced by the night songs of the crickets. Millions of twinkling stars glittered through the unfettered country sky. As we walked back down the gravel driveway, Dave volunteered to lead the rest of us back out to the highway. We said our goodbyes and then headed for home. I followed right behind Dave, keeping equidistance the whole way. He stayed in tune with me, making sure I followed his lead until I got to my exit. I'll never forget what it felt like to leave our connection to head off to my house. I didn't ever want that bond to end. I was so caught. I was so drawn to him. I was so split.

* * *

When I got home that night, I sent an email to Steve and Dave thanking them for suggesting that we go to the Blue Rock. I assured them I too had an appreciation for the energy of the space and the graciousness of the Crocketts, who so generously shared their home with artists and patrons. In response, Dave emailed back:

> *Nancy, I know it was a little outside the box to do a field trip with us, but it turned out to be another spirit-filled night at the Blue Rock. It wouldn't have been the same without you.*

I was glad to receive Dave's email and went to bed feeling a lot of gratitude, excitement, and tension. I was so confused. I couldn't find my way to the truth. I could hear the voice of what I *should* do. And I could feel the longing for what I *wanted* to do. Then there he was again! *The Great Artist* was smiling at me as he invited me to once again move back into the *Studio*.

I got up the next morning, terrified by a foreboding angst. I sat outside on the back porch and watched the birds at the feeder while I wrote everything I was thinking and feeling in my journal. I poured out all my anxiety on paper.

> *I feel so drawn to him and yet so afraid to let myself go there because I am afraid of hurting people, of destroying our spiritual community based on self-serving reasons... Surely, I'm not supposed to break the ethics guidelines for my profession... I could lose my license... I don't want to hurt anyone...*

My anxious prattling morphed into a fervent prayer:

> *Holy Spirit, please guide me. Please give me a clear go-ahead or a clear block. I am so afraid to trust my longing. Bless my movement toward him or block it. Bring me clarity from Your perspective. I so need Your guidance. Thank You for being here...*

While my **Maggie-self** was outwardly writing down all of her angst, my **Nancy-self** was calmly composing an email to Dave. When I finished my frantic journal writing, I went straight to the computer and typed out the email. It just came tumbling out, straight and simple.

I first explained that I had two responses to his email, one from my therapist-self. (In *Dream* terms, this was my **Maggie-self**'s response, still following all of the rules.) This part of me would not have responded to his email. She had already stepped back into the box. I wanted to be sure that Dave knew this. The second response came from a truer, more vulnerable part of me, still outside the box. This was the response my **Nancy-self** could no longer hold back:

> Dave,
> *I loved stepping outside the box last night. The only problem with it is that I feel reluctant to step back inside...*

Then I shared how the *Course* group had become a spiritual community. I was not just the leader of the group, but a member of it as well. Over the years, I had grown to love and respect all of the members. And then I took one more giant step and admitted:

> But here's where it gets hard with you – I feel such a heart connection with you. I so love your tender heart...

Dave and I are both plagued with the same affliction. We both tear up in response to anything that touches us. It is an uncontrollable, immediate reaction to something heartfelt or deeply true. We both do it and we both hate it. And that was one of the reasons I was so drawn to him. I also told him how much I admired his dedication to being more and more open to Spirit.

I ended my email:

> I have found myself wondering today how our lives might have been different had we met at Blue Rock or Starbucks or just in Bob's class. So after spending a few minutes with you on the edge of the box and before I jump back in, I find myself caught up wondering...

Though I wrote the email quickly, once it was complete I found I couldn't send it. I was way too afraid—afraid of making a mistake, of overstepping a boundary, of ruining my *Course* relationship with Dave. I was just flat-out scared. So, I watered the plants. I walked the dog. I did the laundry.

Around 4:00 P.M., I walked over to the computer and clicked *Send*. I did it. No turning back now. This time, I took the X-Acto knife out of **The Great Artist**'s hand and sliced the **Canvas** myself, all the way down the left side and across the bottom, just like I had seen him do so many times before. Oh Lordy! What had I done?! From here, there was truly no turning back. I had sliced the **Canvas** wide open myself, creating **Rupture** Six.

By 10:30 P.M. I still had not heard back from Dave. I was not worried or even surprised; I knew I had thrown him for a loop and he would want to be very careful and thoughtful about his response. At least, that is what I assumed. So, I went to sleep around 10:30 but woke up right before midnight. I walked downstairs, sat down at my computer, and at that very moment, in sailed his response with that oh-so-familiar AOL *You've Got Mail* swoosh that would sound every time Kathleen Kelly opened an email from Joe Fox.

It began:

Dear Nancy,
    This is not the first message I've written to try to explain my thoughts today, so if you get this one before I delete it, another miracle will be born...

After admitting to sharing similar thoughts as mine, Dave invited me to meet him the next day for us to talk about all that we were feeling. I was elated! I was terrified, but now willing to take the risk to see where this would lead. I emailed him back, confessing all of my feelings. In response, Dave wrote: *I'll call you tomorrow. God must be laughing so hard! Good night.*

We both left our computers and went back to bed. Dave called first thing the next morning and we agreed to meet for lunch. He got to the restaurant before I did and greeted me outside with a slight touch to my arm—still no hugs. We entered the lantern-lit glow of the seating area and were led to a private booth where we decided to split a salad, which neither of us touched. Instead, we poured our hearts out as we confessed our mutual attraction and connection to one another.

The conversation flowed easily despite our trepidation. Sequestered words poured out into the space between us like a river breaking through a dam. We felt so familiar with each other and at the same time like strangers meeting for the first time. Dave admitted he had checked into the ethics ruling for counselors and thought at one time that he would leave the *Course* group for two years, and then pursue me on more personal terms after that, but he couldn't ever follow through with it. We both admitted our fear that our feelings would not be shared. So much was unknown.

We were so relieved to finally know that we had been on a parallel track for many years, but at the same time, we were unsure about where to go from there. So, we decided to call our mutual friend and mentor, the teacher of that seminal Sunday school class of so many years ago, Bob Lively, and ask him to help us through this convoluted maze.

QUESTIONS FOR SELF-REFLECTION

1. *Ruptures* by definition expose certain beliefs or assumptions that we have labeled as true but are, in fact, not. If you have experienced a *Rupture* in your life, can you name the assumptions or beliefs that it tore apart? If you have had more than one *Rupture* in your life, did they carry similar themes or were they all different from each other?

2. I have noticed in my own life and the lives of my clients that the intensity of our suffering is equal to the intensity of our resistance to the truth. An example of this was the painstakingly slow start to my relationship with Dave. Can you see ways that this has been true in your own life? What truths have you resisted, and why?

3. How do your particular *Hungry Ghosts* still hold power over you in your life? Do you struggle with how much power you give them or has that struggle calmed down over time? What sorts of experiences re-trigger them?

4. It is important to note that before every one of my *Ruptures*, my *Nancy-self* risked moving out of the *Foyer* and into the *Studio*. How has your *Nancy-self* helped make way for your own *Rupture(s)* to occur?

CHAPTER EIGHTEEN
A TRUE LOVE STORY

You shall know the truth.
And the truth shall set you free.

- Jesus, John 8:32 -

After I got home from my breakthrough conversation with Dave, I called Bob and explained that I was struggling with a professional boundary issue and needed assistance working through it. He agreed to help and suggested that I meet him at his house the following morning. I thanked him and said that was perfect. I did not mention anything more about the nature of the issue, nor did I mention this involved Dave. I then emailed Dave, who agreed to meet me at Bob's.

The next morning, I got there right before Dave did. Although Bob lives in a bedroom community just on the outskirts of Austin, going to his house feels like driving to the country. Houses are secluded from each other by the natural vegetation. No curbs. No streetlights. Bob's house is tucked away in a grove of live oaks and cedars. As I waited, a red cardinal lit on a nearby branch and chirped out his mating call, staccato-style. A warm breeze swirled through the trees, making the oak leaves flutter in the morning light. For a moment, I felt held once again in the quiet, like out at the Blue Rock high above the creek. A squirrel shimmied up the trunk of a nearby oak, another chased right behind, and the reverie was broken. Then, up walked Dave. We walked to the door together.

When Bob came to the door, expecting to see just me, he welcomed both of us without skipping a beat and asked us to come inside. I can only guess what went through his mind at that moment, but he kept his cool and waited for us to explain what had brought us to his door.

After Dave and I explained what was going on, each of us taking a turn sharing our experience of the last nine years together and yet so far apart, I began to spill my internal angst. It flooded the room with an electrical charge. Dave remained silent but attentive. I was imagining him feeling scared, maybe exposed by my unfiltered confessions.

My display of emotion didn't seem to faze Bob. He listened calmly and then simply asked, "Nancy, what is it that you are afraid of?"

I said, "I'm afraid of making a mistake. I'm afraid of losing my license. I'm afraid of hurting Dave and any other client that might be affected by my transitioning my relationship with Dave from a professional relationship to a more personal one. I'm afraid of royally screwing up! I'm terrified!" This, of course, was *Maggie* in full form.

Bob's smile was kind as he listened and became kinder as he began to speak. "Nancy, I am hearing that old fundamentalist religion in you. You are so afraid of making a mistake. Nancy, God doesn't work that way. God is always loving. He never makes judgments. And He certainly does not expect us to be perfect. He wants us to use our time on this planet to explore where love takes us. And I feel a lot of love in this room. Nancy and Dave, ya'll have to pursue this. You can't stop yourselves because you are afraid of breaking a rule. If you want to move ahead and see where this freedom will take you, do it. Don't hold back."

I was both shocked and elated. "I know. I know. I know! I have worked so long and so hard at peeling off the layers of that kind of black-and-white, good-and-evil worldview—and I think I have purged myself of its constraints, its fear and guilt and shame—and then something like this will throw me for a loop and force me to claim and declare which world I really live in. It can be so confusing to me. I feel like I am doing the right thing by living ethically, but I can see that sometimes living ethically restricts my living authentically, restricts my listening and acting on a deeper, more loving guidance." Oh, that *Maggie* is so earnest.

"Ethics are one thing, Nancy, but God would never ask you to strive to be perfect. God wants you to live your life, to risk making mistakes in the pursuit of living the truth," Bob explained.

I knew he was speaking the truth to me and for me. I could *feel* the truth and the love in it. And it felt so freeing. Every cell in my body resonated with his words. I physically recognized them as the truth. My *Nancy-self* had moved into the observer part of me. She was open to really listening, whereas *Maggie* remained frozen in place. As *Nancy* stayed open, she began to allow herself to experience her truth. She began to allow my *Soul-self* to come alive.

Bob continued with a challenge: "So, here's my suggestion. The first thing you need to do is fire Dave as your client and group member."

So, I turned to Dave and said, "You're fired."

Dave smiled and nodded in agreement.

"And then, I suggest the two of you take a two-month sabbatical from each other and use that two months to think and pray and meditate, to continue to ask for guidance from Spirit. But before you start, plan to meet at a certain place, at a specific time. Do not have any communication during these next two months. See if the time apart in prayer and meditation brings you together or not. When you meet in two months, you can share your experience."

Oh my gosh! I realized at that moment that I was reliving *Sleepless in Seattle*. This was just like Annie and Sam agreeing to meet at the top of the Empire State Building before it closed on Valentine's night. I was thrilled by the romance of it all.

Bob's suggestion that we spend some time apart felt appropriate and refreshing and scary and really, really hard. It felt like it would give us that clean break between a professional relationship and a more personal one. We agreed to Bob's plan, both of us trusting we would be guided toward our next step, and left the meeting feeling a new sense of clarity. That didn't remove our angst, but it gave us an underlying solidness that had not been there before. This was a palpable solidity. We both felt it. No words were required.

As we walked back to our cars, Dave said he would call later for us to talk about our plan. He phoned that evening and together we decided to meet again in two months at the Solidago Sanctuary located on the property of the Crossings (now called Miraval), a retreat center located just outside the Austin city limits. We both felt, however, that before we went into silence, we needed to explain to our *Course* group why Dave would no longer be a part of it.

We met with the group as normal the following Friday. I started the session awkwardly. "There's something I need to share with you that is personal. I have realized over the last several years that I have been personally and emotionally drawn to someone in this group but was afraid to acknowledge it out of fear of hurting him and the rest of you. And, that person is Dave."

At that admission, Steve blurted out, "Does he know about this?" afraid that I was just springing this on him.

Dave and I laughed out loud at this and I then assured Steve and the other group members that we had already had a conversation about our situation and had already met with a pastoral counselor to help us work through it. We just knew that we needed to share this information with the group as soon as possible—and I was sorry I had fumbled with the introduction.

After the initial shock, each member admitted that they

had secretly wished Dave and I could be together. It was a natural fit. They could not have been more supportive. Their only regret was that Dave could no longer be a part of our group. They understood that they could certainly maintain a personal relationship with him, but I could no longer be in the role of his group leader.

After that Friday, Dave and I honored our commitment to the sabbatical. We did it and it was excruciating, only making the longing exponentially more powerful. We did just as Bob had instructed—prayed, meditated, and journaled—on our own, with absolutely no contact. As the initial days grew into weeks, I grew stronger in my conviction that I couldn't *not* join this adventure. There is a statement in *A Course in Miracles* that says, "The truth emerges of itself." This dilemma with Dave was allowing me the opportunity to experience what that meant on a visceral level. As long as I was working hard at trying to figure out my truth, I stayed in the conflict. All that got me was spinning in circles of confusion, trapped in the dilemma. When Dave and I consciously took some time off to simply pray and meditate, and journal, it provided just enough space for the truth to come to me. It came as a gift. And when it did, all that was left was an unwavering, felt-sense clarity that couldn't be argued with. I just needed to get out of the way to give it its space. As Jesus had said in the *Jesus Download Dream*, the head is the last to know.

The emerging truth brought with it lots of new insights. Throughout those two months, I began to realize that the issue was no longer about violating an ethics ruling. It had become an issue of either following the truth or living a lie. It was the same dilemma I was faced with in my marriage to Josh. Here I was again teetering on the top of that same choice point—love or fear, truth or illusion—while my Guides gently held a space of complete openness to whatever my *Nancy-self* ultimately chose. There would be no judgment from them with either choice. I was simply being given an opportunity that would determine the next chapter in my life. The choice was all mine to make. It was all up to my *Nancy-self*, the choice-maker inside of me, and she made it based on the truth of her personal experience, not through any kind of rule or formula for life.

On the August afternoon of our long-awaited reunion, it was a sweltering 106 degrees outside. Hot and humid. The air was still and heavy. As agreed, we had had no contact for the duration of the two-month waiting period, so I didn't know for sure if Dave would show up. I knew I had been on an emotional roller coaster since we set up the meeting. Who knew where he had ultimately landed?

Once again, I felt Annie's angst as she rode the elevator up to the top of the Empire State Building where she and Sam had agreed to meet. "Would he actually be there?" she wondered. She honestly didn't know. I didn't either. Dave could have morphed his way back into propriety, for all I knew. He could simply have changed his mind or gotten scared off.

All I knew for sure was that I was there, fully there, ready to risk it all—criticism from others, the fear of making a mistake, breaking a rule, hurting other people. My vantage point had drastically evolved over those two months apart. I knew deep inside myself that they could take my license, but they could not take me. They couldn't take my truth. I would find another way to work with clients if I had to. I was no longer wavering in my commitment to pursuing a relationship with Dave.

Amazingly, all of the critical, doubting voices inside of me had gone completely silent. The *Hungry Ghosts* were no longer taunting. The *Bookkeeper*'s clacking had finally stopped. For me, the two months had served as an incubator for the truth to finally emerge on its own. I don't know that I have ever been that sure or excited about anything else in my life. I had made a full shift from my allegiance to my *Maggie-self* to my truth-based *Soul-self*, exposing once again that when *Nancy* chooses to act from an inner experience of truth, she is shifting her identity to her *Soul*, the part that lives outside of time and space, past all assumptions and expectations, past all the rules and false identities.

I walked down the tree-lined path that leads to the sanctuary and entered through the large, wooden double doors. The room is simple, just an open space surrounded by four glass walls, each exposing a unique natural vista. The air-conditioned sanctuary served as an oasis in the middle of all that Texas heat. When I entered, the room was cool but empty. Dave was not there.

I sat down on one of the leather and chrome Barcelona chairs that sat in the front right corner of the room and waited to see if Dave would come. About six minutes later (yes, I was counting), the doors swung open, and in walked Dave Bair, the love of my life, my sure enough, true male counterpart. I jumped up and ran to greet him. We instantly hugged for the very first time and held on like the long-lost lovers we were, just like Harry and Sally under the disco ball, Joe and Kathleen in the rose garden, and Sam and Annie at the top of the Empire State Building. But this time, it was me—in the flesh, in the here and now, not that perky Meg up on the screen—finally united with my guy.

Dave and I spent the afternoon in that sacred space until dusk. During those magical, miraculous four hours, the details of our lives poured out and intermingled into a newly forming tapestry, the warp and weft of which had, up until that day, been kept in separately wrapped skeins. As the sun started to set, the conversation began to organically slow, both of us wondering where we would go from there. No longer guided by our fears or rules based on collective agreement, we were going to have to trust that life would now lead the way. What we knew for sure was that we felt so close. We had waited so, so long.

As the sun moved closer to the horizon, the conversation came to a natural pause. Dave cautiously looked in my direction and bravely said, "I'm not sure where you are right now. I don't know how to read the timing of this thing. So, I'll just come out and tell you. I talked with the clerk at the reservations' desk before coming over to the sanctuary and found out there are rooms available at the retreat center if you wanted to extend into the evening. I'm not sure how you feel about that."

I sat there quietly for a moment, looking out into the evening sky and then again into those gorgeous blue eyes of his, and said, "Well, I brought my toothbrush."

"So did I," Dave replied.

* * *

Dave and I have barely been apart since that long-awaited reunion. We were married on June 16, 2012, two years and five days after that magnetic evening at the Blue Rock with Eliza Gilkyson singing her heart out while breaking mine wide open. Bob performed the ceremony as we were surrounded by the love and wholehearted support of our extended families.

* * *

Writing this now, some fourteen years after that meeting in the sanctuary and twelve years since Dave and I were married, I have come to realize that love and truth walk right through walls. They don't even see them. We're the ones who keep erecting them, who keep painting more pictures on the *Canvas*. My acknowledging and unabashedly claiming my relationship with Dave gave me another chance to experience this universal law once again, just like the choice to leave my first marriage and just like crossing into the netherworld with Daddy. The Angels, our Guides, those otherworldly beings that live in that undefinable liminal space, neither literal nor just imagined, are with us every step of this human experience—but they never make our decisions for us. They never intrude or impose. They will, however, do everything in their power to point us in the right direction.

I now see that was certainly true with my prolonged journey with Dave. My Guides were with me all along, whispering, nudging, pointing, opening up the space, inviting me to take that X-Acto knife and slash it through myself because this time, they weren't going to do it for me. Just like they did with my dad in the middle of that chaotic psych ward, they gave me the time and space I needed to get there on my own. I just had a hard time believing that love was really real—real for me, that is. I had a hard time believing that Life could be that generous, believing that it wanted to give me what I longed for but didn't think I deserved. The organic Life-Force, posing as all of my Guides in all of their guises, was so much more loving than I could allow myself to be.

That tiny whisper was right all along: *Dave Bair* was the one. He *is* my male counterpart. I just had to catch up to the truth of it by slashing through the **Canvas**—and **The Great Artist** waited with patience, compassion, and trust until I did just that.

QUESTIONS FOR SELF-REFLECTION

1. What do you think about Bob's suggestion that Dave and I take a two-month sabbatical to pray, meditate, and journal about our relationship? Have you ever had to take some time away from a relationship or a project to get clarity around it, to listen for guidance?

2. When I was caught in the confusion and angst about my relationship with Dave, I thought the choice I had to make was between abiding by a rule or violating it, between risking hurting other people or following my heart. What was the real choice about? What does this tell you about levels of awareness or consciousness?

3. In his classic, *Meditations* (1634, first English translation), Marcus Aurelius wrote, "The obstacle is the way." Can you see how that has certainly been true in my life? Can you see how this has been true in yours?

4. The whole struggle with Dave exposes again how my identification with my *Maggie-self* causes me to shrink away from what could bring me more life. The fear of breaking a rule or acting on my behalf, especially with the risk of hurting someone else, are two ways I have leaked out my Life-Force. Can you identify some patterns from your childhood that can still cause you to deaden yourself, leave yourself, or lose your power?

5. Conversely, can you point to some times in your life when you consciously chose to act out of your own experience of truth? What were the effects of that choice?

A DEEPER LOOK #3

CHAPTER NINETEEN
A BIRD'S-EYE VIEW

Once we accept our limits, we go beyond them.

- Albert Einstein -

The Great Artist Dream came to me as a gift of healing some seven years after my first major **Rupture**. Over the years since that gifting, I can truthfully say I have lived the *Dream* and it has lived me. Through all of that living—back and forth—I am still, twenty-four years later, left wonder-struck at its simple elegance, its animated depiction of human evolution in just four scenes: the **Foyer**, the **Studio**, the **Rupture** itself, and the unknown **Space Behind the Canvas**.

But that is not all.

No—now more than ever, I am in love with the climax of the thing, that horrifying moment when **The Great Artist** rips a jagged tear down the side and across the bottom of that electrifying **Collective Collage**. I am in love with *that* moment, the moment in the *Dream* that rattled my bones, gobsmacked me into a no-man's-land of insensibility. I now, some twenty-four years later, through all of the living, back and forth hold that horrifying, grace-filled moment as *The Great Artist's Dream*'s greatest gift to me. And it is this gift I have wanted most to share with you.

This sounds like a crazy thing, to glorify that moment.

Really, that moment?! I know, but I won't shrink away from it.

It was clear from the very beginning that this book was written for anyone who has experienced, just like I have (or maybe far worse than I have), a blow that aches so hard and so deep it leaves you sobbing, huddled on the floor of your bedroom with your heart torn to shreds and your mind turned to mush, screaming, "NOOO! Not this!"

It has been clear from the very beginning that this book was also written for any of you who have experienced, just like I have or maybe far more gloriously than I have, being blinded by a light too bright to see with eyes wide open.

Yes, this book was written for you, but the purpose of this book was not to provide a blanket of comfort for your pain, although that kind of warmth and caring is essential. It was not written to hold you in a downy nest until you can breathe again, although that kind of patience and tenderness is required. Nor was this book written to nudge you into the power of positive thinking, to encourage you to look through the lens of the glass-half-full. It certainly wasn't written to tell you to buck it up, pull yourself together, and get on with it.

No, this book is not about any of that.

The purpose of this book was to look the thing straight in the eye, feel the full brunt of the shock and pain of it, to be humble and raw enough to let the *Rupture* bring you to the end of yourself, to let it take you to the unthinkable, to a place you could never have imagined—*because that is the whole point*. A *Rupture in the Canvas* catapults us right off the ragged edge of our expected, assumed, believed, needed-it-to-be-true, familiar universe and into the infinite, terrifying, creative matrix of life itself. It shamelessly and graciously catapults us right past all of our time-honored, hand-painted images and into the unfathomable truth of who we are and were always meant to be. And that is a ride I didn't want you to miss.

* * *

This is such a hard turn of events to grasp, I know—how a horrific, life-shattering event could somehow take you to the truth of yourself, to some nirvana of a space where it all coalesces into one harmonious whole. Believe me, it's far too big a stretch to get there in one giant step. You have to move over time, sometimes over lifetimes, just like in the *Dream*, from the *Foyer* into the *Studio* and right through the *Rupture in the Canvas* into the Void that waits for you. You have to let yourself evolve from the pre-personal, through the personal, all the way to the space beyond yourself, to the no-longer-personal. Every step is essential to get you there.

I am reminded of the first time I read Thích Nhất Hạnh's *Peace Is Every Step*. The final section called "Interbeing" begins: "If you are a poet, you will see clearly that there is a cloud floating in this sheet of paper. Without a cloud, there will be no rain; without rain, the trees cannot grow; and without trees, we cannot make paper." Hạnh goes on to describe every element he could think of that was required to play its part in the creation of one sheet of paper—the tree, the logger who cut the tree and brought it to the mill, the logger's breakfast that morning, his mother and father, and so on and so on. It took every one of those non-paper elements for this one sheet of paper to exist. But Hạnh doesn't stop there. He goes on to include the reader in the web of elements because it is the reader's perception of the paper that also brings it into existence.

I remember being spellbound by that holistic vision the first time I read it, but I was completely blown away when Hạnh took one more turn of the wheel with his poem, "Please Call Me by All of My Names." Here is a taste of its boldness: "I am the mayfly metamorphosing on the surface of the river, and I am the bird which, when spring comes, arrives in time to eat the mayfly…" But he didn't stop with mayflies and birds. No, not by a long shot. Here's the stanza that hit me like a blow to the stomach: "I am the twelve-year-old girl, refugee on a small boat, who throws herself into the ocean after being raped by a sea pirate, and I am the pirate, my heart not yet capable of seeing and loving."

What sort of trick of the mind do we have to succumb to in order to get to that place of full acceptance of it all, just as it is, with every resistant "NOOO!" stunned into silence? Ahhh, the perfect question. The perfect question that takes us to the stone-cold, dead-end of the thing. Here's the answer: We can't puzzle our way to that level of all-is-well. It truly is beyond us, but it doesn't mean it isn't there.

I hold the story of Viktor Frankl as the best example of that kind of miraculous evolution of mind and heart. For those of you who aren't familiar with his story, he wrote about it in his classic, *Man's Search for Meaning*. Frankl was a Jewish-Austrian psychiatrist and neurologist during WWII. He and his whole family were captured by the Nazis and thrown into separate concentration camps. Frankl was taken to Auschwitz where he lived for the remainder of the war. Upon his capture, Frankl was left with nothing. The Nazis took his home, his entire family, his clothing, and even the manuscript representing his life's work that was sewn into the lining of his coat.

While he was held in the camp, Frankl noticed differences among the prisoners that caught his attention. Every one of them was stripped of everything in their lives, leaving them all on a level playing field. However, their responses to this magnitude of loss were varied. Some of the prisoners gave up and died, some went insane, others joined the guards against their fellow prisoners, and still others saved a crust of bread to give to someone hungrier than they. Frankl asked, "What is it that makes the difference?"

He concluded that what made the difference were the meanings each person attached to his or her situation. He realized that the prisoners who refused to psychologically conform to the mindset of the Nazis in charge, who chose to hold onto their own definition of self, who maintained their own connections to what they valued as true and life-giving, were the ones who were able to thrive in such dire circumstances. In essence, the thriving prisoners' response to the Nazis' attempts to break them was "You can take my clothes. You can take my home. You can take my life's work, even all of my family, but you cannot take me. I get to hold onto me and all that I hold as sacred." But I am quite certain that Frankl was not aware that that level of undefiled clarity lived inside of him at the moment he was stripped of everything he held dear. That kind of unshakableness can only be *discovered* after all of our identity touchstones have been whisked away and only after we have had time to let it all sink in and transmute us into someone new.

During the time that Frankl was held captive, he helped with the plans for escape on four different occasions. Each time Frankl was preparing to leave with the other escapees, right at the last moment, every time, he found that he couldn't bring himself to do it. It's not that he just *decided* not to go. He *couldn't* go. And he couldn't go because he knew that if he did, he would be violating something solid and unwavering inside of himself. It meant that he would be abandoning the weakest and the sickest prisoners, the ones who might not make it if he abdicated his role as a physician. Frankl's *Soul's* calling, his destiny, emerged in the middle of a Nazi prison camp. After everything else was stripped away, all that was left of him was his raw, uncompromising Truth. All that was left was Love. Powerful Love emerged in the middle of hell as Frankl's acorn of fate cracked open into his oak tree of destiny.

But it didn't stop there.

I was privileged to attend the First World Congress of Logotherapy, which took place in San Diego, California, in 1980. Frankl was the keynote speaker. At the end of his presentation, I remember an angry young man stood up to challenge Frankl. In essence, he asked, "I don't understand. Why don't you hate the Nazis? Why don't you want to annihilate them like they did the 1.1 million prisoners that they murdered in Auschwitz?"

I distinctly remember how Frankl responded to the young man's question: "Because I would then become one of them," he replied. That very knowing response exposes that Frankl's destiny was not meant just for him but for the honoring of the whole. My heart still swells with the memory.

Let me be quick to say that although Frankl discovered and claimed his *Soul's* calling in the middle of a concentration camp, thereby allowing him to leave a legacy of truth and depth for the rest of us, it doesn't mean that he would have chosen the details of that rite of passage. I think it would be safe to say that if Frankl could have chosen for himself, he would have preferred that he and his family and his life's work had been preserved in peace and prosperity. Discovering our truest selves on the other side of heartbreak doesn't negate the heartbreak or the very real cherished, personal elements of loss. It just carries the possibility to take us to a place where all the pieces can fit together into a whole new mosaic that we couldn't possibly imagine or, in all honesty, even want to. But by this stage in the journey, it's no longer about what we want or what we thought or even what should have happened to be fair and right and beautiful. It's about stepping into the truest part of who we are, into the essence of our very *Souls*, into our destinies, and then serving out of that deepest truth the only way we can for the whole thing to continue to evolve. What boggles my mind and opens my heart even wider is noticing that a trajectory toward deeper, truer, and more loving is organically built into the process. It's the very nature of evolution. And we as humans get to participate in it if we so choose. Wow!

* * *

So, back to our original questions: What do we do when some unimaginable life event rips through our picture of reality, blows our minds, and breaks our hearts? What do we do when something impossible arises to not only take away a job or a loved one or our health, but shatters who we know ourselves to be, shreds the very fiber of our being—not just rendering us unrecognizable, but completely untethered from all of our identity touchstones? And what about when some unexpected event rattles us senseless with some mind-blowing, heart-opening grace?

From my take on it, those questions can be answered on two levels—1) From the perspective of emotional triage when we are still in the immediate raw stages of the process, and 2) From a more wholistic perspective, which can only be seen and felt after we have reached a new level of equilibrium.

Here is my most compassionate and practical summary of how we are to respond in the immediate aftermath:

1. When your picture of reality is torn to shreds, when your identity is ripped from its moorings, for God's sake feel it. Feel it in every fiber of your being because fully owning the shock or awe of it is a vital part of the journey. Our emotional reactions to these unsettling events expose the foundation we have built our lives upon. Our reactions throw the cover off of our faulty foundational cornerstones.

2. Feel it all fully, but don't stop there. Tell the truth to yourself—that you are undone and you don't know where to go from here. You're lost and clueless. On the immediate level, of course, get all the guidance that you can from seasoned professionals. Get all the help you can from family and friends. Let them bring you a warm cup of tea, a blanket to curl up in. Let them take your kids to soccer practice or out to get a pizza while you sit out on the back porch listening to the birds sing their songs. Whatever you

do, don't do this alone. Surround yourself in a circle of support.

3. On a deeper level, ask the part of you that lives inside of you but extends far beyond you, your Inner Guide, your Inner Council, your Inner Wisdom in whatever form that takes for you, to show you the way out. You are calling upon an aspect of the self that extends far beyond you, that is not bound by your childhood programming, the part that isn't frozen in your fate to show you what you can't see on your own.

4. Stay open, trusting that you will be shown. Start looking for signs and clues—on the inside through insights and intuitions, through dreams and visions. On the outside, look for serendipity, synchronicity or coincidence. Stay alert for clues but don't fill in the blank on how they might appear. Hold fast to that genuine space of "I know nothing. Show me." And when you notice you have lost your way again—which, of course, you will—return to the space of openness and connection; return to trust and curiosity over and over again.

5. And one last thing, have a heart full of compassion and graciousness toward the part of you whose world has been blown apart. It is the only world that part of you has ever known. And then, hold a space of genuine gratitude toward the part of you who is willing and brave enough to learn from it all.

* * *

My second response to those opening questions can only be realized after you have brought a compassionate witness to the bewilderment and the heartache, only after you have asked for all the external and internal help you can gather, only after you have taken some time to let it all sink in and get reworked into the marrow of your bones. After all of that, you can then move into a more reflective and curious relationship with it. It always helps me to go way up high in my imagination and look down on the whole unthinkable thing from that bird's-eye view. From that less personal and immediate perspective, you can then seriously ask yourself, "What was it that caused the intensity of all that pain and shock, anyway?" If you are asking earnestly, it will become obvious that it wasn't solely from the actual loss of whatever it was that you so cherished. While there's no need to diminish the pain on that level, in truth, the intensity of the pain and the shock is equal to the tenacity of your hold on what you cherish that causes the **Rupture**. You assumed that that thing or person or job or house or system of government or your health or [fill in the blank here with your own experience] would be there forever or be healed or protected from danger or, at the very least, turn out differently from the way that it did. *Our greatest pain comes from life violating our take on things.*

If I take a bird's-eye view of my most painful **Ruptures**, the loss of my first marriage, for example, I can now see that I had been holding onto the marriage out of fear that I was not worthy of Josh's love and devotion. It was my own inner fears and mistaken assumptions with their corresponding images painted on the **Canvas** that kept the marriage together. The wrenching pain of my marriage's ultimate dissolution hit when I finally allowed the truth to take precedence over the painted images. The marriage needed to go. It was already gone. But when that truth began to emerge, my first response was to kick and scream. This is what caused me the most pain, which has now, years later, been replaced with gratitude for the whole tumultuous ride.

And what about the intensity of the pain that I felt when my dad had to be committed to the psych ward? With that one, I couldn't breathe. It was so egregiously unacceptable to me. It was so, so wrong. In my mind, he didn't belong there! And there's the clue—"In my mind..." Daddy being restrained among people with severe mental degeneration was not an image painted on my *Collective Collage*. That violation of the way things were supposed to turn out was what caused my protective daughter's heart to break apart. With that one, it didn't take me too long to stop and go inside myself, to call upon that inner Voice of Loving Wisdom to show me a different picture. And when I asked, it spoke to me from a place of understanding that pried my heart wide open. It painted a picture of my father and where he was on his path that I could never have come up with while focused on my *Ruptured Canvas*. When I heard the truth, I instantly surrendered and moved into a place of perfect harmony with it. I would gladly play my part for him as he played out the part of himself that could not let go of his control of life.

Now, let's bring this back to you. I can imagine the sorts of life events that would bring you to read a book like this: the loss of a child, a partner with a debilitating disease, barely surviving a natural disaster, losing your home, being betrayed by a dear friend, experiencing a serious injury. On the level of the actual loss, any of these experiences would be more than enough to cause any of us to become undone by them. That kind of response is normal and to be expected. But if you look more deeply at the real cause of the pain, a new layer of truth can emerge. We only assume that our children are supposed to outlive us. We could never have imagined our partner suffering a debilitating disease or ourselves being the victim of a natural disaster, losing our home, a friend betraying us, or experiencing a serious injury. None of these experiences was supposed to happen. They weren't images painted on the *Collage*. And because of that, our whole identity gets yanked out from under us. It leaves us angry at Life or God. It leaves us kicking and screaming because these sorts of things weren't ever supposed to happen. And because they have, we are left powerless and bereft.

But let's stop and notice what is going on here from an even wider perspective. To do this, we have to go back to Thích Nhất Hạnh's description of interbeing. The bird didn't eat the mayfly because it had a vendetta against it. Eating the mayfly wasn't a personal attack. Life wasn't punishing the mayfly. The bird ate the mayfly because it was lunchtime and he was hungry. To fully understand why the bird ate the mayfly, we would have to travel back in time and examine all of the elements that had to coalesce in that one particular moment for that bird to eat that mayfly, just like Hạnh showed us how all of the non-paper elements were required to play their parts for the piece of paper to come into existence. The bird ate the mayfly because a whole host of factors tumbled into that one encounter in that one moment between that particular mayfly and that particular bird. What we are talking about here is the nature of reality. How it all really works. *Reality does not conform to our preferred picture of how we would want it to be.*

It gets more complicated when we are talking about the twelve-year-old girl who throws herself into the ocean. Why did this happen? How could this happen? It's so, so, so wrong. It violates every fiber of our being. But the truth is it happened just like the mayfly and the bird. Every one of those cascading elements—everything that happened to that twelve-year-old girl before she jumped into the ocean—the circumstances of her birth, her age, her gender, her nationality, all the reasons she was fleeing her country, how she ended up in that particular boat on that particular ocean—as well as everything that happened to the pirate up until the moment he chose to rape her—his upbringing, his level of self-esteem, all that went into his decision to join that band of pirates on that particular ocean, his level of consciousness, all the tragedies and triumphs of his life. It took every one of those cascading elements for that one encounter to happen between them.

And the same thing is true about Frankl and his ending up in a Nazi concentration camp—his brilliance, his nationality, the era in which he lived—in tandem with all the elements it took to shape Hitler into the deranged dictator that he became, and all that went into the making of a whole culture of people who allowed themselves to get caught under his spell. Frankl's captivity wasn't personal. On the level of the human heart and in all that we believe about justice, this should never have happened to Frankl or anyone else. But it did happen. And it happened because they were all caught up in the madness of their times. The Nazi regime clearly played out in history the only way it could. And Frankl was one captured element in that whole dehumanizing unfolding. That is the truth of the thing. That's the reality of it. Reality isn't personal, although it affects us all in the most intimate and poignant moments in our lives. Reality isn't fair according to our human understanding of the word. It happens the only way it can, given the whole set of moving parts that put it all into play, all the ones that we can see and all the ones that are hidden from our view. Ah, the hidden ones bring in the backdrop of mystery that pervades the whole shebang. It is that hidden mystery that takes us past all words, past our ability to piece it all together.

We get upset when reality doesn't conform to our very idiosyncratic notions of how it should play out. Our distress exposes our narcissistic stance on life. And that's how we all respond when we are living in either the *Foyer* or the *Studio* of our psyches. It's only after a life-altering *Rupture* that we can begin to get a more realistic perspective on the whole thing. That doesn't happen overnight. It is an ever-evolving process.

So, where does that wholistic level of recognition take us? It doesn't bring back the dead, it doesn't restore us to health or rebuild a friendship or our tornado-blown house. More often than not, it leaves us with the loss. The *Canvas* isn't repaired. But a new world emerges behind it. If we can open ourselves up even a tiny bit to the space of unfettered possibility right past our broken hearts, a new way of being can be brought to our awareness—one that isn't dependent on a hand-painted image; one that recognizes that this thing we are all in the mix of is multi-layered. So much of it is hidden from our normal way of looking at things. Discovering this inexhaustible layer of awareness changes our entire relationship to Life. It takes us out of the driver's seat and puts us in a position of deep humility where we can be receptive. And from that position, Life's Benevolence, its creative take on things, can surprise us into a whole new realm and a whole new sense of self. At least, it has for me, layer by layer.

* * *

Simply put, on the front side of the *Canvas*, a *Rupture* always comes as a shocking violation—at the very least, as a loss of our hold on things. On the *Back Side of the Canvas*, a *Rupture* carries with it a potential gain, but in a form we could never, ever have predicted. On the *Front Side of the Canvas*, we spend our time and energy trying to cram reality into a four-sided frame. On the *Back Side of the Canvas*, right in the middle of our lowest moment, the Life-Force-of-the-Universe, with a twinkle in his eye and a smile on his face, gently says, "Hey there, come over here. There's something amazing I want to show you."

QUESTIONS FOR SELF-REFLECTION

If you have had enough distance from your life-shattering events—only after you have exhausted your need to kick and scream, only after you have allowed all the feelings to be expressed and held with compassion—think back on all that you have gone through and write down what you've discovered along the way.

1. Start by making a list of all the images on your *Canvas* that were taken from you. What got ripped away or shredded into nothingness? Then note what you found on the other side of that devastation. What new awareness, perspective, or questions arose for you on the *Back Side of the Canvas*? Here's a clue: *Awareness happens spontaneously when what is blocking it is removed. When our picture of reality is ripped open, the truth emerges of itself.* (Although, this can certainly take some time.)

2. Are you aware of your current overriding life lesson? If so, can you see how each of your *Ruptures* has reinforced it? If not, stay curious about it.

If you aren't in a position to do this just yet, no worries, but keep this exercise handy for a time when you think you are. Remember Rilke's advice to the young poet: *Have patience with everything that remains unsolved in your heart... At present, you need to live the question. Perhaps you will gradually, without even noticing it, find yourself experiencing the answer, some distant day.*

CHAPTER TWENTY
A PARTING GIFT

*Driven by forces of love,
the fragments of the world seek
each other so that the world may
come into being.*

- Teilhard de Chardin -

As I contemplate what final words I want to leave you with, I know I don't want to use my rational mind to come up with them. I am through with analyzing. No more trying to explain. Instead, I want to end by connecting with that liminal space one last time.

I close my eyes and sit still and quiet. I stay open to what might come next...

I am surprised by an Inner Vision. In the silence, a kaleidoscope, just like the one I saw after Daddy was admitted to the psych unit, appears once again in my mind's eye. An exquisite mandala arises in my inner vision, a mandala made up of tiny shards of colored glass, visible through a pea-sized channel of light. I see how each shard fits perfectly with every other to create a pattern of beauty far beyond that which any of the individual shards could evoke on its own. And yet, I am aware that this exquisite mandala wouldn't exist without each one of the individual shards holding its place, allowing itself to be a willing conduit for the shimmering light.

In the background, I hear that familiar Voice reminding me of all the lessons my *Soul* has learned so far. As the color-filled imagery evolves in my mind's eye, I hear a Voice reminding me of all that has come before. There is no break between them. Together, the imagery and the reminders are creating the whole felt-sense experience.

As the light-filled mandala glistens in front of me, I hear *The Great Artist* once again ask his enticing question as he pushes open the flap in the *Canvas*:

"So, Nancy, what are you going to do with that?"

I smile in appreciation of his bold playfulness.

As I hear that now-familiar question, one slight turn of the light-infused cylinder sends all of the shards tumbling topsy-turvy out of sight, landing once again into an equally elegant but different pattern, each shard tossed into a new but equally valuable place within the oneness of it all. As I watch, the whole thing just keeps going around and around, spinning in space like a sparkling thing of wonder.

As the shards fall in and out of place, I notice that some of them land in the foreground, and others fall out of sight. It is clear to me that each of the colored shards, whether visible or hidden, continue to play their particular part. They support each other, collapse, and support again as the next exquisite, interconnected pattern emerges.

I hear my list of familiar prayers echoing around me—*Maggie*'s, *Nancy*'s, and my *Soul*'s:

"NOOO! Help me! Help me! Help me!" *Maggie* pleads.

I hear *Nancy*'s humble request: "*I know nothing. Show me.*"

And then my *Soul*'s petition, "*Help me to be a conduit of love in this space.*"

I fall in love with the fervency of each of them.

As I keep my gaze on the current mandala before me, I am bathed from every direction in multi-colored light, encapsulated just like the panoramic *Collective Collage* in the *Studio*. But this animated tableau is not stagnant in time and space. This one is alive with its movement and its pauses, with all of its transitions and creative new arrangements. Once again, I realize that each of the mandalas is playing its part for every other light-filled pattern, just like each of the tiny shards of glass plays out its part for every other shard and every other larger motif. And through their improvisational interconnection, they are co-creating one exquisite wholistic pattern after pattern.

In the background, I hear the voice of Jesus whisper in my ear:

"Nancy, hold still, I am downloading something. We don't have time for me to explain it to your head. It will be the last to know."

This makes so much more sense to me now. I am filled with gratitude.

In the background, I hear the Voice reminding me of what it told me during my past-life regression:

"His life lesson was life-death-life-death. Yours is: LifeLifeLifeLife."

I remember how surprised I was at that revelation. I had no idea what it meant. There is so much that I am still learning.

Then out of nowhere, I realize that this interconnected spiral that I am swept up into is taking me somewhere. It is taking *all of us* somewhere. We are all going together and our togetherness is expanding outward in every direction as we go along. As the mandalas spiral outward, their patterns become more and more inclusive and more and more intricate all at the same time. All of us are graced by their palpable elegance. We are individually and collectively being brought into this whole evolutionary thing of elegance and beauty, of chaos and confusion. But through all of its unsettling twists and turns, through all of its seeming losses and all of its realized gains, through all of its sacred pauses, each of us and all of us are willingly surrendering into it—none of us in control of it. Each of us and all of us are willingly playing our parts in this grand, organic, cosmic dance. Each of us and all of us are giving into it and being gifted by it, as well.

Ah, but even that is not the end of it. I see that there is more.

The Voice breaks through the silence again. This time with Daddy's final words on his way out.

"*I love you, sweetheart.*"
"*I love you, too, Daddy,*" I say in return.

As my heart is rekindled by my father's final words, the imagery surrounding me expands wider still. I recognize that I, like each of us, am not only one of the shards, nor am I just a part of the whole pattern of beauty and chaos; I am also the one observing it all. I am the one witnessing all of the shards tumble and land, tumble and land. I am the one recognizing its aliveness as it spirals out into eternity. And with my focused watching, I, now as the observer, am also gifted by it all. Ah... I, as the witness, am playing my unique part in it too, as the one who notices and the one who tells its story.

I smile again as I hear in the background Dave's hesitant yet oh-so-bold question to me in the sanctuary, as well as my response:

"*I'm not quite sure where we go from here. I found out from the receptionist in the Retreat Center that there are rooms available if we want to continue into the evening.*"

"Well, I brought my toothbrush," I replied.

I can't help but laugh. My *Soul* quickens to the sound of his words as I am brought back to the light-filled space that surrounds me. But then, I realize there is one more wider vista still. And this one couldn't possibly be left out. For this one more wider perspective includes you, My Reader Friend. Of course it includes you.

Through all of this writing and sharing, through all of this showing and telling, you have been right here with me. Not a moment has gone by without my feeling your presence sitting next to me at the keyboard. I have been writing for myself, of course, to integrate all of my particular, personal **Ruptures**, but more importantly, I have been writing for you, seeing myself as one who is eager to bring compassion to your fears, as one who willingly holds a space of trust when you scream "NOOO!"—as one who knows from her own experience that those shocking turn of events you may find yourself in can take you someplace beyond your imagination. I have been writing from the truest version of myself that life has called me to be—as a midwife, one of them at least, to your emerging *Soul*. But here's what so delightfully weaves the whole thing synergistically together. You, with your presence, with your listening and receiving, have simultaneously served as the midwife to mine. I thank you.

With much love and gratitude from my heart to yours,
Nancy

APPENDIX

THE DREAM AS ROADMAP: OVERVIEW

Before describing the specific details of the *Dream*, it is essential to recognize three overriding characteristics:

1) Every element in the *Dream*—each character, each space, and each transition between the spaces—represents an aspect of my personal psyche. However, in the descriptions to follow, I have generalized them as representations within the human psyche in general, not just specific to mine.

2) Each variable plays a defined part in the whole and is therefore essential to the full storyline.

3) The overall movement in the *Dream* exposes a developmental progression—*the evolution of consciousness*, which is set into motion by a life-stopping event. What will become clear throughout the narrative is that each physical space in the *Dream* (**Foyer, Studio**, the **Rupture** and the **Space Behind the Canvas**) represents a different level of awareness or consciousness characterized by how the primary characters, **Maggie, Nancy**, and **Soul** (see descriptions below), hold themselves in relation to a particular authority figure—the **Hungry Ghosts** in the **Foyer**, the egoic-self in the **Studio**, or the **Great Artist** who invites us to follow him through the gaping hole in the **Canvas**.

The movement in the *Dream* was a major revelation to me.

It surprised me by placing those mind-blowing, heart-stopping events in our lives within a developmental progression, within a predictable pattern. It no longer defined them as merely out-of-the-blue, isolated, shocking somethings in desperate need of healing, but very deliberately placed them into a wider context in relation to our preexistent picture of reality. The movement in the *Dream* exposes how our reactions to these events are outer expressions of how we see ourselves within our version of reality. It portrays a life-altering event as a violation of our picture of reality, leaving us with a choice: to either cling to the defiled picture or to let it go and trust where life will lead from there. The latter option takes us past all preconceived ideas or images, right off the edge of the *Canvas* into an undefined, open space.

The climax of *The Great Artist Dream*—that unexpected *Rupture in the Canvas*—jangles our relationship to truth. It turns our worlds upside down by revealing what we thought was true as false or, at the very least, limited. What we first experience as an unredeemable disaster gets exposed as a secret doorway into Benevolence.

I am quite aware that this can be a pill too big to swallow at this point. But stay with me.

The Key to the Roadmap

The following is a summary of the vital role each element of the *Dream* plays in relation to all the other parts and to the whole evolutionary process. *The Great Artist Dream* is the roadmap we follow throughout the book. This summary is meant to serve as the key to that map. Read through it now to get a glimpse of the journey, and then use it as a reference point as you read the chapters of the book.

You will notice that I have fleshed out some of the elements from the *Dream* based on my experience with them over the last two decades.

The Characters

1) The *Maggie-self*, represented in the dream as *Nancy*'s friend, is the part of us that has come along with *Nancy* to study under *The Great Artist*. *Maggie* is an identity adopted in childhood that is based on survival and has been programmed to believe certain things. Her survival is best served by conforming to the energies, expectations, and pressures that surrounded her in her formative years (i.e. the *Hungry Ghosts* [read on] in the *Foyer*), as well as the limitations and mistaken assumptions that she brought with her from her past life experiences (if reincarnation fits your worldview). *Maggie* is the holder of all of our fears, blocks, and limitations. She shows us where we are restricted and stuck. Regardless of the form she takes in each individual life, the *Maggie* part of the self is always fear-based.

Maggie always places her trust in the authority of the *Hungry Ghosts* as well as the corresponding images on the *Collective Collage* painted by the others before her. *Maggie* never thinks for herself. She is just an extension of what she has been taught, having no real existence beyond the influences of the *Hungry Ghosts* and the pre-existing images on the *Canvas*. If she adds anything to the painting, it will be an image that is consistent with those that were painted by those who came before her. She would only paint an image that she thinks others would admire or approve of. In other words, *Maggie* is incapable of original, creative thought. In contrast to *Nancy*, *Maggie* does not grow and evolve. She deserves our compassion but not our allegiance.

2) The *Nancy-self* is the part of us that carries agency, the one who has the power to choose, who has free will. In psychology, we would call this part the ego, which is characterized as a separate sense of self.

Nancy is the part of us that can choose how she wants to

respond to each of *The Great Artist*'s invitations throughout the *Artist's* warehouse—unlike *Maggie*, who only accepts the invitations if doing so allows her to remain identified with her childhood programming.

When *Nancy* chooses to paint her own images on the *Canvas* in the *Studio*, she can do so through four different perspectives: 1) Through her self-focused ego, which paints images that only serve herself in some way without regard for anyone or anything else. This part is divorced from the whole; 2) Through her analytical, problem-solving mind, where she works hard at figuring out the best, most accurate, or smartest images to paint; 3) Through experimenting, getting curious and creative, trying out some novel ideas, and seeing where that takes her. This is an expression of the freedom she allows herself, unlike the programmed *Maggie*; or 4) Through painting images that seem to represent the uniqueness of who she believes herself to be, to the best of her ability to discern it. This is a powerful part of the evolutionary process when *Nancy* is beginning to experience a strong sense of a separate self. This is not the same as her *Soul*, but it is far more authentic and more conscious than either her conforming *Maggie* or her purely self-serving ego.

Once a *Canvas* is ripped, however, it is once again up to *Nancy* to decide how to respond. She can abdicate her role as a choice-maker and align herself with *Maggie*'s automatic, fear-based reaction. She can delude herself into believing that she can find a way to repair the *Rupture*. She can choose to deny its existence and continue to paint images around it, or she can surrender to the recognition that she has lost all control over the situation. This moves her into a position of genuine humility, with the admission: "I don't really know who I am or what truth is. I'm all out of images." From there, *Nancy* can accept *The Great Artist*'s invitation to venture outside anything she has ever experienced or could even imagine. All four of these perspectives provide **Nancy** with different experiences of herself and life. If she is paying attention, she can learn and grow from each of them.

When the **Nancy-self** chooses to follow **The Great Artist**, i.e. the Creative Life-Force, she is put in the position to work in tandem with the **Soul-self**. (Keep reading for more on the **Soul-self**.)

3) The **Soul-self** is not a visible character in the **Dream**. She emerged into bold relief the moment **Nancy** stepped through the **Canvas** for the first time. The **Soul-self** and the **Nancy-self** may experiment with working together before the first major **Rupture**, such as in moments when we make decisions for ourselves based on a deep inner knowing, going beyond what any outer authority would have us do. This is when **Nancy** is very much intact, but she is not acting egotistically. She is tapping into something inside herself. Maybe her karma or an aspect of her **Soul**'s calling. It gets hard to put these experiences into distinct categories, so bear with me as I try. Examples of this cooperation in my life are when I decided to go to graduate school or when I decided to leave the church of my childhood. Neither of these choices was associated with a major **Rupture** in my life, but they were times when my **Nancy-self** chose to paint images consistent with my inner truth. They were not predetermined by the pre-existing images painted on the **Collage**. However, consistent with the **Dream**, it is true that my **Soul** was made most evident to me on the **Back Side of the Canvas** after the first **Rupture**. When that happened, my **Nancy-self** blew up. That was the first time I recognized such a clear distinction between the self I knew myself to be—a combination of **Maggie** and **Nancy**—and a self that was far bolder and truer than either of those could ever dare to be on her own—my **Soul**.

I have come to experience the **Soul** as the part of us that is eternal and always in alignment with truth. She accompanies us through every lifetime. The *Soul* is the part of us that continues, undiminished, after death, retaining all the life lessons that are learned through each incarnation. Of course, I can't prove any of this. These definitions have arisen purely from my lived experience.

The *Soul* emerges gradually when *Nancy* is inspired by a deep inner knowing to make a unique addition to the *Collective Collage*, and more drastically every time *Nancy* chooses to step through a new *Rupture in the Canvas*.

4) The *Three Hungry Ghosts* are the combination of the *Bookkeeper* and his two invisible sidekicks, the *Preacher* and the *Protector*. Like the *Soul*, the sidekicks are not visible in the dream, but their presence is viscerally felt in the *Foyer*. Like lions at the gate, they stand on either side of the double swinging doors that lead into the *Studio*. The trio's collective job is to try to keep *Nancy* and *Maggie* from entering the *Studio* where they might act on their own. The *Hungry Ghosts* act as the inner representations of the outer authorities from childhood.

In my life, the *Preacher* is the voice of "be good" or "be perfect" and the *Protector* gives the constant warning to "be careful" and "play it safe." It is the *Bookkeeper*'s job to keep track of when we are following those authorities' demands or when we are violating them. Once we are adults, the protective intentions they served in our childhood end up sucking the life out of us by keeping us small, afraid, guilt- and shame-ridden, and, most importantly, under their control. *Nancy* dares to ignore their warnings by either acting on her own, listening to her deep intuitive truth, or choosing to step through the *Canvas*, while *Maggie* gives into them every time. Let me emphasize that the *Hungry Ghosts* serve as a necessary incubating and socializing container during childhood but become a hindrance to growth and individuation in adulthood. (For a fuller description of a related theory, see Richard C. Schwartz's work on Internal Family Systems. Start with *No Bad Parts* {2021}.)

5) **The Great Artist** is our wisest inner Guide. He is the part of us who encourages the *Soul*'s expansion, who continues to invite us into both the freedom of the *Studio* and the creative mystery that lies behind the *Canvas*. He is always respectful and honors both **Maggie**'s fear-based refusal to move forward and **Nancy**'s freely chosen participation in the journey. He is a personified form of the Creative Life-Force, of our Inner Reservoir of Unconditional Love and Divine Wisdom. In the *Dream*, **The Great Artist** is expressed as masculine, but in life, the Inner Reservoir of Unconditional Love and Divine Wisdom shows up as equally feminine or non-binary.

The Spaces:
Levels of Consciousness

The contained spaces in the *Dream* represent three levels of consciousness designated in Transpersonal Developmental Psychology as pre-personal, personal, and trans-personal. The uncontained opening caused by the **Rupture** is a transitional space. (For a comprehensive explanation of the evolution of consciousness, read anything by Ken Wilber. Start with *No Boundary* (2001).)

1) The **Foyer** represents the pre-personal (preconscious) aspect of the self, which is always governed by an outside authority yet becomes internalized over time. In the *Dream*, this room is drab, gray, lifeless. It is also foreboding. It does not feel safe in the **Foyer**. It is anything but welcoming. This is where the **Hungry Ghosts** watch over us, flanking the entrance to the **Studio**. (The reasons my **Foyer** carries these characteristics are explained in detail in Chapter One.)

2) The *Studio* represents the personal level of awareness. This is the land of the ego, the experience of the separate self. The *Studio* is where my **Nancy-self** gets to make all of her choices. The *Studio* is associated with the analytical mind, self-will, and personal imagination, but it is also the place where **Nancy** can choose to surrender all control. Although **Maggie** follows **Nancy** into the *Studio*, she brings along her dependency upon the authority of the **Hungry Ghosts**. She is too afraid to avail herself of the real freedom that is offered to her in this new space.

The amazing *Collective Collage* is displayed and encountered in this room. It includes a combination of the paintings of all of the people who have come before **Nancy** and **Maggie** and provides an opportunity for them to add images of their own. The painting is seen as an illustration of everything up to this moment in time that one might imagine, dream, assume, believe, desire, dread, aspire to, abide by, run from, or move toward. It is experienced as truth, as reality. Although much of it was painted by others, it represents both **Nancy** and **Maggie**'s personal pictures of reality.

When **Nancy** and **Maggie** enter the *Studio*, it appears that they are both looking at the same *Collage*, but because the meaning that it holds for each of them is based on their separate levels of consciousness, they are experiencing two different images. In other words, the *Collage* is unique for each of them based on their relationship to it. Both **Nancy** and **Maggie** are mesmerized by the array of images on the *Collage*, but **Maggie** sees it as a complete picture of reality—a collection of images to choose from. To her, reality consists of what others have painted for her, which in her mind sets the limits to what is possible. **Nancy**, on the other hand, sees it as the totality of images painted by those before her, but also as a space for her to delve into her own imagination, thoughts, and ideas—to participate with it, to add her unique touch to it, not just to accept it as all there is to life. To **Nancy**, the *Collage* is an opportunity to explore who *she* believes or experiences herself to be in relation to all the other images, as well as from a space of truth that lives inside of her. Until there is a **Rupture in the Canvas**, the experience of *truth* is mediated through **Nancy**'s perception of what that might be.

To **Nancy**, the **Studio** is where all the magic happens. To **Maggie**, the **Studio** is a holding place for all that life has to offer.

3) **The Rupture in the Canvas** is an opening that serves two purposes. It both defiles the **Canvas**, which is what makes the **Rupture** so shocking and often painful but it also provides the portal that exposes the **Space Behind the Canvas**. The **Rupture** is what brings about the choice point between either seeing it as simply an overwhelming destruction of something that **Nancy** and **Maggie** valued and assumed to be real, a disaster to rail against—OR, after the initial shock, recognizing it as a doorway to someplace completely unknown. The **Rupture** represents the transition between the personal level of awareness and the unimaginable, transpersonal level of awareness that lies just beyond the mind's ability to comprehend.

4) **The Space Behind the Canvas**, which I often refer to as the **Back Side of the Canvas**, represents the supra-conscious or transpersonal aspect of the self. With **The Great Artist** as a guide, this space leads into the indefinable mystery, into a pregnant emptiness that requires both deep humility and at least the size of a mustard seed worth of trust to enter. The admission price is a willingness to surrender control. Choosing to enter it always leads to greater awareness, despite the ego's reluctance to let go of its hold on things. In this space, life is discovered. It is not something to be figured out or even imagined.

The **Space Behind the Canvas** is the alchemical matrix in which the Divine invites us to partner with it.

The Transitions Between Rooms: Three Invitations, Three Responses

1) The *First Invitation*, which in the dream was the invitation to come and study under *The Great Artist*, is the choice to incarnate into this lifetime—to come to the Earth schoolroom to learn life lessons. It begins with our physical birth. Acceptance of this invitation leads us into the *Foyer*.

2) The *Second Invitation* is to become a unique self with personal choice and agency. In the *Dream*, this second invitation was extended when *The Great Artist* invited *Maggie* and *Nancy* into the *Studio*—"Ready to come on back?" This represents the birth of the ego or a separate sense of self. The transition between the *Foyer* and the *Studio* always requires willing participation. *Nancy* and *Maggie* both accept the invitation but on different terms. *Maggie* is eager to move into the *Studio* and wants to add her own images to the collage, but she does not avail herself of the full opportunity offered to her there. *Maggie* can only experience herself as a separate person in terms of inhabiting her own unique body and experiencing her own unique history, but she does not give herself permission to think for herself. Her mindset stays within the restrictions of the authorities of her childhood. *Nancy*, on the other hand, enters the *Studio* with a sense of openness and genuine curiosity. It is important to note that *Maggie* remains the constant companion of *Nancy* in both the *Foyer* and the *Studio*. Where they are separate from each other is in their personal experiences of each of the spaces, and most dramatically when *Nancy* chooses to step through the *Rupture in the Canvas* and *Maggie* stays behind, horrified by it.

3) The *Third Invitation* comes in the form of *The Great Artist*'s question as he opens the flap in the *Canvas* at the end of the

dream: "So, what are you going to do with that?" This question invites both **Maggie** and **Nancy** to step into a space of nothingness, no images, no words, no concepts.

Maggie stays focused on the destructiveness of the **Rupture**. **Nancy**'s acceptance of this invitation leads her into the **Space Behind the Canvas**, into a direct encounter with life, no longer mediated by assumptions, images, beliefs, or expectations.

The Direction of Movement

The movement in the dream is an evolutionary process that begins in the **Foyer**, leads into the **Studio**, goes through the **Rupture**, and finally opens into the **Space Behind the Canvas**. The entering of each space comes through a conscious choice. With each invitation, the Creative Life-Force continues to invite us toward greater expansion, but it is up to us to accept each invitation or to stay where we are. In the *Dream*, **Maggie** prefers to stay in the mindset of her childhood programming, whereas **Nancy** claims her right to personal agency, first by going into the **Studio** to paint her own images, and secondly by choosing to surrender everything to follow **The Great Artist**'s lead. Moving into the **Studio** and stepping through the **Canvas** both lead to an expansion of the self—one through an incremental, gradual awakening and the other through an abrupt eruption.

It is important to note that although the *Dream* presents this process as a seamless, ever-expanding forward movement, in our waking lives the unfolding of this evolutionary pathway is not linear. It always involves fits and spurts, two steps forward and five steps back, identifying with shrinking **Maggie** in one moment, with willful **Nancy** in the next, but eventually, if we dare to get curious, if we dare to trust the process even the slightest little bit, we can find ourselves merging into alignment with our **Soul**'s identity. For most of us, though, it doesn't end there. Most of us inevitably step back into the *Foyer*, where we are hoodwinked by the insatiable *Hungry Ghosts* all over again. Although it may look like it and be experienced as such, this whole meandering process isn't just willy-nilly. This uniquely human evolutionary trajectory can take us somewhere far beyond, deeper and wider, more loving and more true than we could possibly imagine on our own. This uniquely human evolutionary trajectory can take us to the miraculous if we dare to accept its invitation.

REFERENCES

BOOKS

Aurelius, Marcus. *Meditations*. Translated by Gregory Hays. New York: Modern Library, 2002.

Conroy, Pat. *The Great Santini*. New York: Dial Press Trade Paperback, 2002.

Foundation for Inner Peace. *A Course in Miracles*. 3rd ed. 2007.

Frankl, Viktor E. *Man's Search for Meaning*. Boston: Beacon Press, 2006.

Hạnh, Thích Nhất. *Peace Is Every Step*. Edited by Arnold Kotler. New York: Bantam, 1992.

Hendrix, Harville, and Helen LaKelly Hunt. *Getting the Love You Want: A Guide for Couples*. 20th anniversary ed. New York: St. Martin's Press, 2007.

Meade, Michael. *Fate and Destiny: The Two Agreements of the Soul*. Seattle: Greenfire Press, 2012.

Rilke, Rainer Maria. *Letters to a Young Poet*. Translated by Charlie Louth. London: Penguin Classics, 2011.

Schwartz, Richard C. *No Bad Parts: Healing Trauma and Restoring Wholeness with the Internal Family Systems Model*. Boulder, CO: Sounds True, 2021.

Webb, Wyatt. *It's Not About the Horse: It's About Overcoming Fear and Self-Doubt*. Carlsbad, CA: Hay House, 2003.

Wilber, Ken. *No Boundary: Eastern and Western Approaches to Personal Growth*. Boulder, CO: Shambhala Publications, 2001.

SONGS

Gilkyson, Eliza. *He Waits for Me. Beautiful World*, Red House Records, 2008.

— *Requiem, Paradise Hotel*, Red House Records, 2005.

— *Sanctuary, Hard Times in Babylon*, Red House Records, 2000.

Kool and the Gang. *Celebration. Celebrate*, De-Lite Records, 1980.

Jorgenson, E.L. *Almost Persuaded. Great songs of the Church: Number Two*. Colorado Springs, CO: Standard Publishing, 1937.

ACKNOWLEDGMENTS

Although writing is a solitary endeavor, it takes a whole community to transform a rough draft into a published book. Some within that community offer direct support to the writing process. Others offer their support through family ties or friendships. *Rupture in the Canvas* has been blessed with both.

This final version of the book would not have been written had I not read Kelly Notaras's *The Book You Were Born to Write*. Thank you, Kelly, for encouraging me and so many others to walk past our fears and straight to the keyboard.

I am grateful to my first editor, Neva Knott, for holding me accountable every step of the way through the first draft. That was a major hurdle. I give my heartfelt gratitude to my developmental editor, Kathryn Chandika Liedel (see wordsbychandika.com) for not only her experience and expertise but, more importantly, for her intuitive ability to meld into that ineffable creative space with me. That was a gift of both her brilliance and her wisdom.

Special thanks to the talented crew at Atmosphere Press for escorting me over the finish line. Their easy, welcoming manner, author-centered approach and professional expertise as creatives and technicians could be felt through all aspects of the project management, final editing, as well as the layout, cover design and marketing consultation. Big kudos go especially to Alex Kale who served as the Project Manager for the whole production. Alex was the point person for all the elements from beginning to end. Much gratitude also goes out to each of the specialty heads and their crews: Guy Bierman, Tammy Letherer, Erin Larson, Chris Beale, Dakota Reed, Ronaldo Alves, Kevin Stone, Matthew Fielder, Karli Fitzgerald and, finally to Evan Courtright for his guidance throughout the recording and distribution of the audio version of the book

Once we were on our own for the independent, author-recording, Kirk Wheeler who works for a private production company in southern California stepped in to serve as the Audio Engineer. His experienced feedback was invaluable. My son, Jacob Cunningham (aka Jack) graciously agreed to serve as the Production Manager for the author-recording. Gleaned from years as a Senior Live-Action Director, Jacob seamlessly wove together his fine-tuned technical savvy, unwavering patience and natural warmth. He held my hand, coached me through the rough spots and cheered me on through every step of the way. "Be still, my Momma heart."

Words fail when it comes to expressing how grateful I am to my circle of friends for simply loving and believing in me: A group of lifelong women-friends who met when our children were young but who have stayed friends through our shared values and our connection of the heart—Ann Calvert, Sarah McBride, Nancy Fike, and Sharon Bates. Dr. Sara Dennis falls into this category as well, but she also graciously served as a beta reader for one of the working drafts, offering insightful feedback. I am equally grateful for Karen Prewitt, Suzanne Clark, and Jayne Clarke, three women who were divinely placed on my path during those tumultuous last years of my first marriage. That connection is still strong today.

I deeply appreciate the time-honored roles that Dr. Bob Lively and Dr. Frank Allen have played in my life as mentors, colleagues, and friends. Each in his own way not only nurtured my therapy practice but my spiritual evolution as well. In that vein, I can't put into words how grateful I am to my clients throughout the years. Although we play different roles, in some ineffable way, we always become students and teachers to each other.

This page cannot hold the fullness in my heart for all the support my family has surrounded me with during all my years of writing draft after draft. My sisters, Elizabeth (Betsy) Davis and Robyn Whyte, the other two legs of our three-legged stool; and my children, Emmie, Cade, and Jack. It's not easy to have a close family member write about the most vulnerable aspects of your shared history, but each of these brave and gracious ones has whole-heartedly supported me as I have done just that. Not only have they been my greatest supporters, but each allowed the reading of *my* perspective of our family history as an opportunity to share some of *their* memories or *their* personal take on what all of it meant to them. These conversations have been priceless and an unexpected bonus to the writing.

Not enough can be said about the love of my life, Dave Bair. He could not have created a stronger foundation, a safer container, or a more loving presence for me to pour everything I have learned and experienced throughout my lifetime out onto the page. His patience has been Job-like as I have taken up residence in our breakfast room-turned-writing space, relegating him to watching his golf matches or UT games, his contract writing, or client phone calls to our upstairs bedroom. But beyond those logistical concessions, Dave has been my confidant, my cheerleader, my best friend, and my most ardent supporter. He has embodied the term "Soulmate" beyond anything I could have imagined. He continues to show me what true love is.

In the larger arena, I am grateful to Dave's children, Sierra and Will, for graciously welcoming me into their family and sharing their dad with me –to Sierra for always extending her tender heart and to Will for never failing to make me laugh with his quickest of wits. I am grateful to our beloved golden retriever, T-Bone, who slept on the floor behind my desk chair as I typed every page. And lastly, I cherish the nature trail that I walk every day, as it continues to hold me in its sacred space.

ABOUT
ATMOSPHERE PRESS

Founded in 2015, Atmosphere Press was built on the principles of Honesty, Transparency, Professionalism, Kindness, and Making Your Book Awesome. As an ethical and author-friendly hybrid press, we stay true to that founding mission today.

If you're a reader, enter our giveaway for a free book here:

SCAN TO ENTER
BOOK GIVEAWAY

If you're a writer, submit your manuscript for consideration here:

SCAN TO SUBMIT
MANUSCRIPT

And always feel free to visit Atmosphere Press and our authors online at atmospherepress.com. See you there soon!

photo credit: JKC Images

ABOUT THE AUTHOR

NANCY WILLBERN, PhD, has been a transpersonal psychotherapist in private practice for nearly three decades. Fascinated with the intersection of psychology and spirituality, she thinks of herself more as a midwife to the Soul than as a traditional clinician. A condensed version of the chapter "Splintered Pieces" was published in the January/February edition of the journal *Spirituality and Health*. Willbern lives with her husband just outside the Austin city limits on the edge of the Texas Hill Country. For more, visit nancywillbern.com.

www.ingramcontent.com/pod-product-compliance
Lightning Source LLC
LaVergne TN
LVHW041907070526
838199LV00051BA/2529